Peak Di Boundar, walk

190 miles around the edge of the national park

Edited by Andrew McCloy

Love the Peak?
Help us protect it

Peak District Boundary Walk
190 miles around the edge of the national park

First published in 2017 by Friends of the Peak District.

Friends of the Peak District,
37 Stafford Road, Sheffield S2 2SF, United Kingdom.
www.friendsofthepeak.org.uk

A CIP catalogue record for this book is available from the British Library.

ISBN 978-1-909461-53-6

Front cover: Buxton and beyond. Photo: Tim Mackey.
Back cover: Green mist. Photo: Villager Jim.

All maps reproduced by permission of Ordnance Survey on
behalf of The Controller of Her Majesty's Stationery Office.
© Crown copyright and database rights 2017 OS 100058185.

Design and production by Tim Mackey.

Printed and bound by Pulsio in Bulgaria.

MIX
Paper from
responsible sources
FSC® C128169

Contents

Foreword

Can you imagine anything better? A walk around the entire Peak District National Park, all 190 miles of it. I adore circular walks, but this one beats them all. The joy of circumnavigating one of Britain's best-loved landscapes and our oldest national park can't be anything other than deeply satisfying.

The walk itself is through beautiful countryside, along carefully chosen footpaths, tracks and quiet lanes that wind along the boundary. This is a chance to experience, whether you take the walk on as a whole or in sections, each of the special landscapes that make up the national park: the 'bite' that takes out the huge limestone quarries but exposes us to the delightful limestone dales; the rougher, wilder landscape of Macclesfield Forest; the hidden delights of the Roaches; a peep into Dovedale; the pleasure of Matlock's hills and dales; the glorious freedom of the Sheffield edges; a yomp across the Pennines; the striking urban edge landscapes which look into Oldham, Stalybridge and Glossop; and finally Kinder itself, its glorious majesty crowning the experience. Though there are, as a result, continual tantalising glimpses to better-known interiors, this is a perfect way to experience the Peak District's special setting, and to walk in the footsteps of those who campaigned to make national park designation a reality.

Because the Peak District boundary was chosen and scrutinised with enormous care, since the earliest days of the Campaign for National Parks, the Peak District was a prime candidate. But what to include and what not? How to choose its edge without diminishing the importance of those lovely moors and dales that had to be excluded? As always, it was our forebears who had the courage and determination to make those judgements and deliver a boundary that has stood the test of time remarkably well.

It is now nearly 90 years since Ethel and Gerald Haythornthwaite first tramped these hills and valleys in search of the right boundary for the Peak Park. Their recommendations fed directly into the work of the Hobhouse Committee, which in turn provided the foundation for the National Parks Commission's work when they developed and consulted on boundaries back in 1950. Today's walk does not follow the national park boundary slavishly, but gives us treat after treat in seeing the Park from and through its edge, the chance to discover little-visited nooks and crannies and to appreciate some of our best loved landscapes from a new perspective. Enjoy!

Dame Fiona Reynolds
President, Friends of the Peak District

Introduction

The Peak District was formally designated as Britain's first national park in 1951, but this landmark moment followed several decades of campaigning by conservation and recreation bodies who argued that areas of special landscape value needed national protection. The Standing Committee on National Parks was established as far back as 1936 and its volunteer ranks included the Council for the Preservation for Rural England (represented locally today by the Friends of the Peak District). However, even before this, a group of campaigners, led by the Friends' founder, Ethel Haythornthwaite, had already drawn up a proposed boundary for a national park in the Peak District which turned out to be almost identical to the one we have today.

The Peak District National Park covers 555 square miles (1,438 sq km) and is one of the most accessible and popular of our 15 national parks, reaching into the counties of Derbyshire, Cheshire, Staffordshire and Yorkshire, as well as the urban fringes of Sheffield and Greater Manchester. To celebrate this diverse and special place, and to reflect on a long and close association with the Friends of the Peak District, a new 188-mile (302km) long distance walk has been devised which follows the boundary first drawn up by the Haythornthwaites all those years ago.

The route stays as close as possible to the edge of the national park, following existing paths, tracks and quiet lanes, as well as the occasional former railway line and even a canal towpath. There's also an 'alternative' moorland section between Longdendale and Dovestone Reservoir if you fancy a more serious upland challenge, as well as plenty of scope for using the route as a springboard for wider exploring. In so doing, the Boundary Walk enjoys a wonderful mix of Peak District landscapes and different terrain - from dramatic crags, cloughs and open moorland to quiet woodlands, pasture and hidden dales. There are views aplenty and also the space and freedom to enjoy its tranquillity. One of the reasons for creating the route was to raise awareness of the Peak District's outstanding natural beauty and to encourage people to cherish and protect it. Walkers will find themselves away from the crowds and popular hotspots of the Peak District, as the Boundary Walk seeks out less well known paths and quieter corners of our first national park.

The production of this book has been a truly collaborative project. After mapping the approximate route on paper, volunteers walked it on the ground and made many improvements using their local knowledge. They have helped shape it in every way, from agreeing the criteria for the route and the conventions for the written directions, to the photos used to illustrate it. They also wrote the articles about conservation issues and the Friends' campaigns to protect the stunning landscapes it traverses. A huge thank you to all those volunteers who gave up their time for this highly original project.

How to explore the Boundary Walk

Long distance walkers may enjoy the challenge of walking all 188 miles in one go, but the route has been divided into day stages which are more accessible to walkers who prefer to explore the Park boundary in manageable day-long walks. The stages have been designed so that they start and finish at locations convenient for public transport connections, car parks, toilets, local shops, cafes and pubs; but given the sometimes remote nature of the Peak District, this hasn't always proved possible. Although the route is shown on strip maps throughout the book it is always advisable to carry a map of the area in case you want (or need) to change your course; and don't forget to go equipped for the conditions you're likely to encounter, since some of the route is across high and exposed ground.

However you choose to enjoy the Peak District Boundary Walk, whether you dip into it for a day or an afternoon or tackle it continuously over a fortnight, the route is a reminder that our national parks are a source of inspiration, relaxation and recreation for millions of people. The historical significance and the sheer quality and variety of the Peak District landscape makes this national park particularly special, but, as the articles throughout the book make clear, it needs constant vigilance and hard work to keep it this way. For 90 years the Friends of the Peak District has been safeguarding this treasured landscape for the future, by encouraging others to enjoy, understand, value and protect it. We hope it inspires you.

Enjoy your walk along the boundary!

Route planner

Stage	From	To	Miles	Km	Ascent feet	Ascent metres
1	Buxton	Peak Forest	10.2	16.4	983	300
2	Peak Forest	Hayfield	9.7	15.6	1326	404
3	Hayfield	Old Glossop	9	14.5	1432	436
4	Old Glossop	Greenfield	9.8	15.8	1576	480
5	Greenfield	Marsden	10.6	17	1959	597
6	Marsden	Holme	8.5	13.7	1523	464
7	Holme	Langsett	10.5	16.9	852	260
8	Langsett	Low Bradfield	10.5	16.9	1346	410
9	Low Bradfield	Ringinglow	9	14.5	1508	460
10	Ringinglow	Millthorpe	9.3	15	964	294
11	Millthorpe	Beeley	10.6	17	1121	342
12	Beeley	Winster	6	9.6	1198	365
13	Winster	Roystone Grange	10	16	1083	330
14	Roystone Grange	Thorpe	7.7	12.4	567	173
15	Thorpe	Waterfall	8	12.9	1086	331
16	Waterfall	Tittesworth Resr	11.4	18.3	1094	333
17	Tittesworth Resr	Wildboarclough	10.1	16.2	1174	358
18	Wildboarclough	Bollington	8.5	13.7	1532	467
19	Bollington	Whaley Bridge	9.5	15.3	1363	415
20	Whaley Bridge	Buxton	9.2	14.8	1216	371
Totals			188	302	24,903	7,590

The Boundary Walk and the Peak District National Park

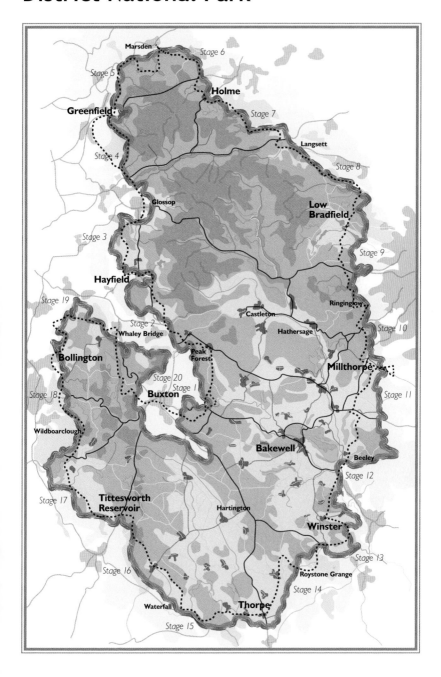

Marsden
Stage 6
Stage 5
Holme
Greenfield
Stage 7
Langsett
Stage 4
Stage 8
Glossop
Low Bradfield
Stage 3
Stage 9
Hayfield
Stage 19
Ringinglow
Castleton
Stage 2
Whaley Bridge
Hathersage
Stage 10
Peak Forest
Bollington
Millthorpe
Stage 20
Stage 18
Stage 1
Buxton
Stage 11
Wildboarclough
Bakewell
Beeley
Stage 12
Stage 17
Tittesworth Reservoir
Hartington
Winster
Stage 13
Stage 16
Roystone Grange
Stage 14
Waterfall
Thorpe
Stage 15

Oaken Clough from Mount Famine

Buxton to Hayfield

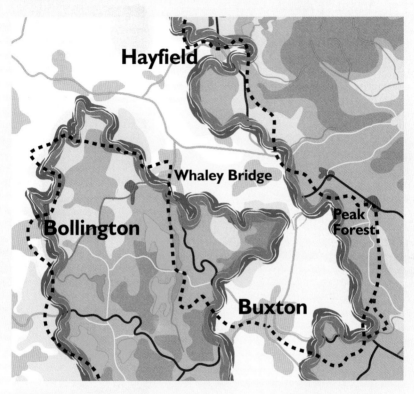

The Walk begins in the elegant spa town of Buxton, famous for its period Georgian architecture, but very soon it heads into the Peak District countryside and plunges into tucked-away limestone dales rich in wild flowers. From the banks of the River Wye it's a stiff pull up on to the open and rolling pasture above, with expansive views as the White Peak turns to Dark and the more rugged gritstone scenery replaces the softer limestone. Now the Boundary Walk rolls up its sleeves for a high-level route across the Peak District's lofty western shoulder, with Kinder Scout looming large, via an exhilarating stretch of the Pennine Bridleway which ends in the attractive village of Hayfield.

Stage I
Buxton to
Peak Forest

Start: Buxton Town Hall (GR SK 058733)
Finish: Peak Forest (GR SK 113793)
OS map: Explorer OL 24 The Peak District – White Peak Area
Distance: 10.2 miles/16.4km **Ascent:** 983ft/300m

Peak Forest

Paths and terrain: Grassy field paths and a few steep, sometimes rocky slopes. The alternative section via the stepping stones in Chee Dale should only attempted if the river levels are low and the conditions are safe.

What to look out for: Deep Dale and Hay Dale are delightful nature reserves, rich in limestone-loving native plants and wildlife and often dry in the summer months; while the deep wooded valley of Wye Dale and the gorge of Chee Dale makes for a dramatic passage alongside the River Wye. At Wormhill a memorial commemorates local lad James Brindley, inventor of the modern canal system, while glimpses of quarries past and present are a reminder that this is still a worked landscape.

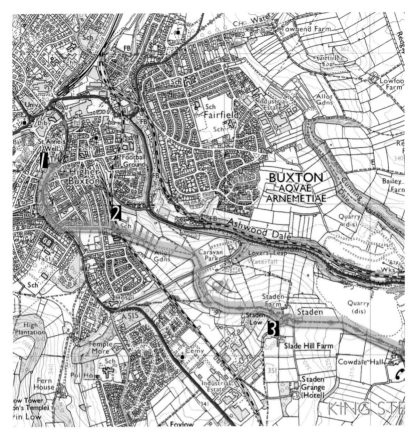

I From outside Buxton Town Hall in the market place head south down the High Street, go across the 5-way traffic light junction towards Ashbourne and take the second turning on the left into Byron Street. Continue to the end (crossing Kents Bank Road) and follow a footpath sign on the right over a railway bridge.

2 Walk ahead through allotments as far as a gate, then continue ahead next to a fence on the right, with Ashwood viaduct on the right. Head towards a double telegraph pole, go through a gate/gap in the wall and then turn immediately right and head steeply downhill to the road. Cross the stile and walk ahead through Lime Tree Caravan Park (middle road), uphill past some farm buildings and through a farmyard before bearing left up the hill on a grassy lane. Pass through a gate and continue left up the hill to the hamlet of Staden.

3 Go through Staden following the footpath signs. Cross a stile on the right and follow the track over stiles to the back of some farm buildings, finally emerging on the road at Cowdale. Turn right on to the road, for a stile on the left. Now walk across the field to a gate on the right, then continue through a further three gates to reach a road near to King Sterndale church.

4 Turn left on the road and take the Midshires Way through a gap in the wall on the right. Walk ahead through fields and into Deep Dale, bearing right for the steep zig zag path to the bottom of the dale. Here turn left and follow the path through the dale. Go down steps and take the path on the left near the interpretation panel. With Topley Pike quarry now on your left, follow the fenced path to finally emerge on the busy A6.

5 Cross the road and walk through the car park along the vehicle track all the way to Blackwell Mill. Follow the path with the river on your left past the bike hire centre and Blackwell Mill cottages. Cross the bridge and turn right.

From here the main route follows the Pennine Bridleway out of the valley to Wormhill, but for a more adventurous option see the 'stepping stones alternative' route described on page 16.

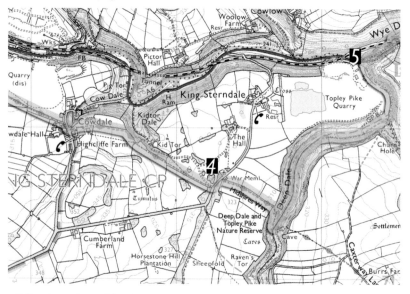

6 Go along the trail by the river until the Pennine Bridleway sign. Go left uphill on a zigzag route. Turn right at the top through Mosley Farm farmyard. Turn left on the road for 500m to the first public footpath on the right. Go through a narrow gate and cross two fields towards Flag Dale. Drop down a very steep stony path to Flag Dale and up a similar path on the other side. Cross two fields diagonally right to reach Hassop Farm, where you join the road into Wormhill.

7 Continue through Wormhill on the lane to the crossroads. Turn right, then where the road bends sharply right take the trail straight ahead and follow it down to Dale Head Farm and into Hay Dale via a wall stile.

8 Continue to the end of the dale, over the stile and turn right onto the road. Take the footpath on the left just before the road starts to climb. Follow the footpath along Dam Dale, with the wall on your left over stiles and broken walls, until reaching the back of a farm with sheds to your left. Go through the gate and to the stile ahead. Turn left at the stile, signposted Dam Side, across a field as you contour around the hill to reach a small white house.

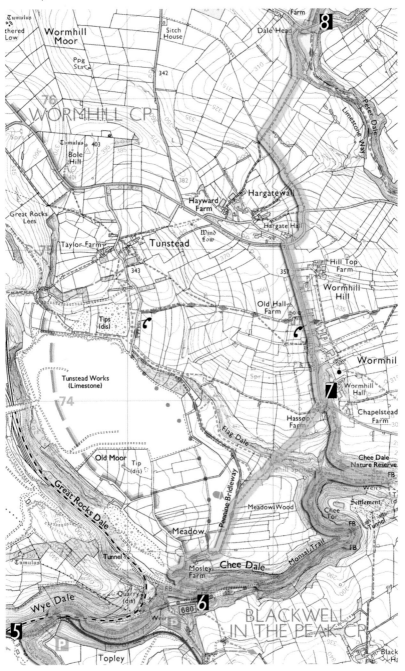

9 At the tree by the white house go through double gates, then at the signpost on the corner go left, over the right hand stile. Walk forward uphill to the gate at the top on the left. Go through the gate and follow the wall on your right until you reach the road.

10 Turn right on the road and proceed past New House Farm until you get to a T-junction. Turn right and walk along the road to Peak Forest.

A stepping stones alternative

At the end of point 5, follow the path beside the river into Chee Dale and via stepping stones through the dramatic gorge. Continue along a sandy and wooded section, then at a footbridge turn left and double back up steeply through a small wooded ravine to reach the lane for Wormhill.

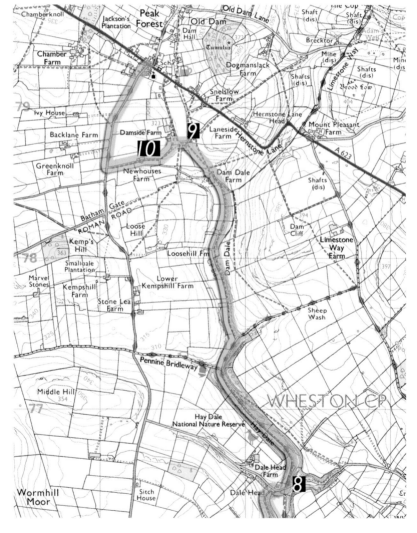

Stage 2
Peak Forest
to Hayfield

Start: Peak Forest (GR SK 113793)
Finish: Hayfield (SK 036869)

OS map: Explorer OL 1 Peak District – Dark Peak Area and OL 24 Peak District – White Peak Area

Distance: 9.7 miles/15.6km **Ascent**: 1,326ft/404m

Hayfield ©David Toft

Paths and terrain: Undulating field paths and bridleway tracks, mostly firm underfoot, but note that as you cross the pasture west of Peak Forest there are few signposts and the route is not always clear.

What to look out for: Peak Forest was once the centre of the Royal Forest of the Peak, and Chamber Farm (now rebuilt) held the Forest Courts. Near Slackhall is the Chestnut Centre wildlife park, famous for its otters and owls. The second half of the stage beyond Chapel-en-le-Frith follows the switchback Pennine Bridleway.

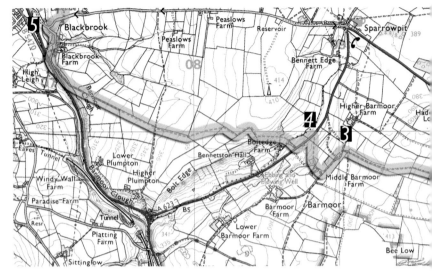

I Leave Peak Forest crossroads on the A623 towards Sparrowpit for 200m. To avoid the main road, walk around Chambers Farm. Take the footpath on the left and cross three fields diagonally right (no visible walked route). At the top right hand corner of the third field there is a narrow corridor field passing in front of Chamber Farm on your right. Keep close to the wall on your right and continue through several fields. When a grassy track comes in from the left, turn right through a gateway in the wall, heading down towards a small building by the road. Look out for an easily-missed step stile on the left.

2 Now gently climb through successive fields, where disused pits are an indication of previous open-cast mining, while ahead is the steep-sided Bolt Edge. Finally when you are in line with a group of trees, pick up a hardened track downhill to a T-junction.

3 Turn left and on along the track to Middle Barmoor Farm. Turn right over the stile (to the right of the farmyard gate). Keep the farmhouse to your left and cross another stile before reaching the road.

4 At the road, turn left and cross (with care) to a stile on the right. Head downhill, cross a stream in a ditch, then uphill, towards a clump of trees. Veer left through gorse to small gate at top. Keep close to wall on left and after sharp left turn take stile in wall ahead. Continue through more fields, to a signpost with four directions on it, including straight on for Blackbrook. Follow this track dropping down towards Blackbrook, until it runs into a better road, briefly running alongside the A6 for a short stretch. At a tarmac lane walk through the hamlet of Blackbrook to the end of Blackbrook Lane. If you want to visit Chapel-en-le-Frith turn left, under the A6 flyover. Otherwise turn right.

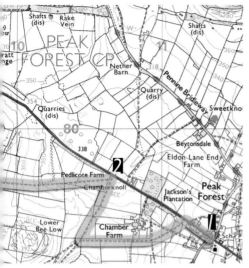

5 Walk 30m up the road until you reach a signposted footpath up steps on the left, (opposite prominent steps on the right). Cross the field, go diagonally right to cross a wooden footbridge and turn right. At the track turn left to reach a road. Turn left down the road and immediately take a signposted footpath over a wooden stile on the right. Cross the field to the right of the wood where there's a gate and follow the footpath sign to Wash, past the rear of Bowden Hall.

6 At the road turn right and follow it up the hill as far as Bowden Head Farm. At the T-junction cross the road, go through a gate and continue along a path to another gate. Follow the path through a plantation of trees. At the end of the trees go through a gap and walk downhill close to a fence on the right of the field. Walk to the bottom of the field and cross a footbridge over a stream. Follow a track diagonally left uphill to reach a gate and short path to the road. Turn right and walk uphill past Roych Farm.

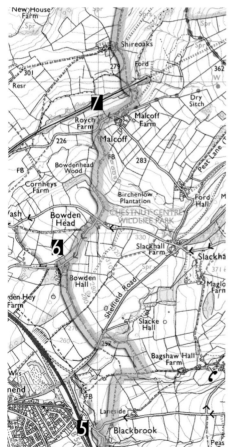

7 At the footpath sign on the left of the road, go through two gates to reach a grassy track down to the railway line. Cross the bridge, go through a gate and walk uphill diagonally right to the corner of the wall. Continue up the hill, past Shireoaks Farm, with the wall on your left.

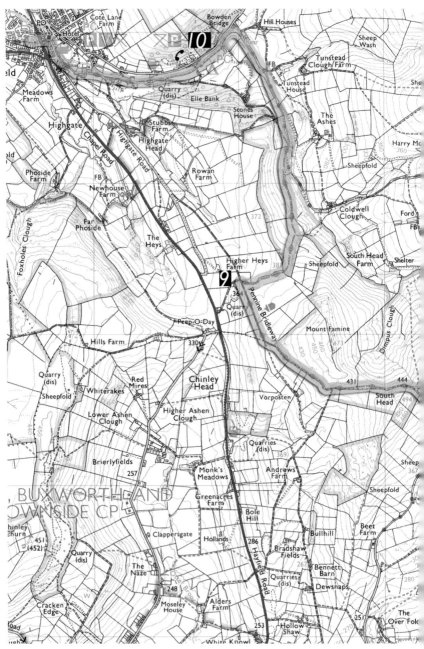

8 When you reach the Pennine Bridleway turn left and walk this route along to South Head (you can make a detour onto South Head itself) and Mount Famine. Continue on the bridleway through a gate and continue to walk downhill. Go through a set of three gates and continue ahead on the bridleway.

9 At a crossroads with a signpost to Kinder Valley, turn right and walk along the bridleway. Go through two gates and walk downhill to a metalled track at the bottom. Turn left and follow the track until you join a road at a cattle grid. Go left, downhill, on the road to a stream and crossroads, then turn left and follow the stream towards Hayfield.

10 Walk into the campsite along the drive, then go to the right of the campsite along the banks of the river onto Valley Road. At the end turn right onto the main street of Hayfield.

Kinder Downfall from Mount Famine

Ethel riding her horse Bracken in her beloved 'stone country'

Pushing the boundaries

Contrary to the media myth, our national parks did not come about simply because of the Kinder Mass Trespass of 1932. The idea of national parks dates back to Wordsworth in the early 1800s and then began to take hold elsewhere in the world, notably in the USA where the first to be created was Yellowstone in 1872. After stop-start progress in Britain from the turn of the 20th century, public pressure became more focused in the 1930s when CPRE, the Ramblers and the YHA formed the Standing Committee for National Parks, now the Campaign for National Parks, to argue the case.

In November 1938, a group of organisations, including CPRE, the Ramblers and the Peak & Northern Footpaths Society, met at the Church Hotel in Edale (now The Rambler Inn) to begin the campaign for the Peak District National Park. Also present was John Dower, the civil servant whose work laid the bedrock of the 1949 National Parks Act. His advice was clear and firm: properly worked-out proposals and strong local support would give the best chance of early success.

The Edale meeting had been convened by Ethel Haythornthwaite, the founder and leading light of CPRE in the Peak District (which later became Friends of the Peak District). She had already been taking soundings nationally on whether the time had come to campaign forcibly. Although CPRE nationally had misgivings (with the approach of war) she pressed ahead. The group (by now the Joint Committee for the Peak District National Park) met again in Edale in early 1939, this time to task volunteers with a section by section survey of the proposed boundary. In an uncanny echo of history, 77 years later this Boundary Walk was also stitched together and refined by a group of dedicated local volunteers.

Of course, there were problems

along the way.

The East Cheshire branch of CPRE initially objected to the western fringe being designated, but were talked down by John Dower. More difficult was the schism with those solely supporting national park status for Dovedale, led by Frederick Holmes, the chair of the Buxton Committee of CPRE. Happily, Dower (who was tasked with bringing forward the first round of proposed parks) favoured the same wider Peak plus Dovedale scheme that was being promoted by Ethel's Joint Committee.

Hobhouse boundary map

The next hurdle, once the National Parks Act was passed, was to defend the Joint Committee's boundary at inquiry when the government proposed a smaller area. By this time, the prize of being the first national park to be designated was uppermost in the Joint Committee's mind. Under pressure from the Inspector, some of the areas originally proposed (notably around Brassington and Bradbourne) were let go, rather than face interminable wrangling and delay. Finally on 17 April 1951, the Peak became the first national park, due in no small part to Ethel's vision and determination to force the pace.

The boundary has surely stood the test of time and is largely as we would wish it. No serious attempts have yet been made to enlarge it, although the exclusion of the moors east of Stalybridge and Mossley (where the boundary follows the edge of Lancashire, which was politically opposed to the Park) is surely the biggest anomaly in landscape terms. Sadly this omission has also led to this beautiful area being blighted by the pylons that bestride the moors between Tintwistle and Stalybridge.

Ethel Haythornthwaite née Ward

Gravy Pud fell race from Tintwistle

Hayfield to Greenfield (Dovestone Reservoir)

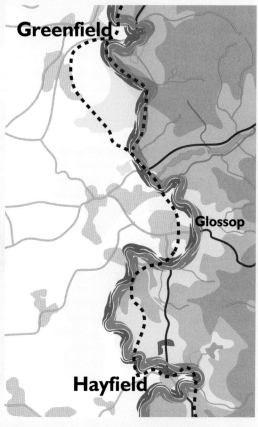

Continuing its steady progress northwards, the route weaves an undulating course below the high moorland of the Dark Peak, with Bleaklow towering impressively above. Despite this, there's a strong human influence on the landscape lower down, with old mills, reservoirs and well-established transport routes all evident, most keenly felt when the Walk dips down into Glossop and then Longdendale. Both are staging posts on two of the main trans-Pennine routes that cross the national park, still making headlines today as we ponder issues of sustainable travel. The final part of the section approaching Saddleworth includes the option of an adventurous and high-level moorland crossing, with both routes coming together to end below the dramatic crags that ring Dovestone Reservoir, near Greenfield. However, although the wild and bulky moorland seems to frame every view, the proximity of Greater Manchester is a reminder just how closely urban and rural lines are drawn.

Stage 3
Hayfield to Old Glossop

Start: Hayfield (GR SK 036869)
Finish: Old Glossop (GR SK 041948)
OS map: Explorer OL 1 Peak District – Dark Peak Area
Distance: 9 miles/14.5km **Ascent:** 1,432ft/436m

Hayfield from Lantern Pike

Paths and terrain: There are poor paths and few signs around Rowarth, so careful navigation is required, and also take care crossing several busy roads. This is another hilly stage, with some sharp slopes and long pulls.

What to look out for: This undulating traverse of the national park's north western boundary includes several fantastic hills and ridges, beginning with Lantern Pike above Hayfield, with its 360 degrees viewpoint. Approaching Glossop there are more great vantage points, including Cown Edge and Whiteley Nab. The stage finishes in Old Glossop, the historic part of the town centred on All Saints parish church that retains much of its charm and character.

1 From Hayfield Bus Station walk along the Sett Valley Trail towards New Mills. Pass the reservoir to a gate onto a road.

2 Turn right on the road, pass a crescent of houses on your right and café on your left. Immediately after the houses, take a cobbled track uphill on the right to a road. Turn right on to the road and immediately go left on a path (signposted Pennine Bridleway) uphill to a gate. Go through the gate and immediately left, steeply up to Lantern Pike, following the path along the edge to the trig point.

3 Continue past the trig point downhill to rejoin the bridleway and reach a gate. Go through the gate and take the left path, following the wall on your left for 600m until you reach a wide track. Turn left on to the track and go through a gate. After 500m, as the track bends left, take the stony walled route (a restricted byway) down on your right. Follow this into Rowarth.

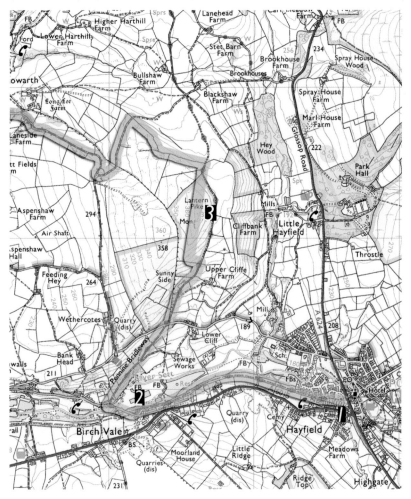

4 From Rowarth, take the first right turn on the lane alongside houses. Continue to the road and a row of houses by an old phone box. Take the road in front of the houses and turn right at a T-junction, then almost immediately left on a footpath with signs for Cown Edge. Follow the path uphill over several stiles and cross a wide walled track. When the grassy track flattens out head for a metal gate. Go over the stile at the side of the gate and then diagonally right uphill across the field, then over several stiles. The Edge flattens and after crossing a wide track a wall is reached above Rocks Farm to the right. Fork right, with the farm below, and stay high on the edge passing a quarry on the right. Take the fenced path on your right after the quarry to Monk's Road.

5 Cross the busy road with care (blind bend) and go through two small wooden gates and head towards the right of the wood on a faint path past Whiteley Nab. From the corner of the wood there is no path, so go half right and descend until reaching an iron gate. Pass through the gate and down the overgrown path to a stile/gate on the left. Go past Herod Farm on the left. Follow the road until the road junction (there are many paths here, so care is needed with navigation).

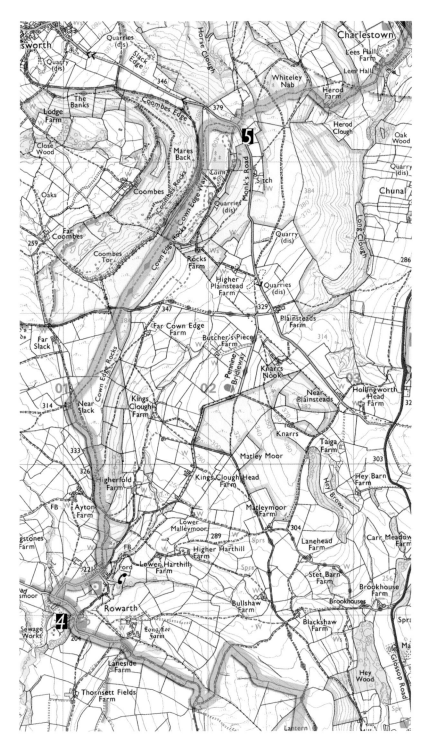

6 Turn right and walk to the T-junction (A624 Hayfield-Glossop road - take care when crossing). Turn left and walk towards Glossop, past old factory buildings, and take a lane directly behind the factory. At the top of an incline, after passing a house on the left, take a footpath uphill to a road. Turn right at the top, then take the first footpath on the left up steps into a field, before reaching houses.

7 Walk uphill, on the right fork, on a faint path to the field corner where a shrine usually contains various trinkets. Go over a stile and follow the fenced path along the road-edge of the field, with superb views southwards.

8 Pass in front of two cottages and start to descend on the path, with views of Bleaklow to the right. Descend the field northwards, ignoring paths left and right.

9 At the road turn left and follow it downhill to a bridge with a bridleway sign on the right and into a housing estate. Take the bridleway on the right to go alongside the river. Cross a footbridge and up onto the road. Go left past the bus stop as far as the bend, then cross onto a wide path. Cross the A57 at the traffic lights, then turn left, back over the river, and go first right at a sign for Manor Park. (To access Glossop town centre simply continue along the main road.)

10 From the entrance to Manor Park take the first footbridge over the stream and follow signs to the café and toilets. Pass the bowling green and walk to Manor Park Road. Turn left to the Queens Arms pub, then up Church Street South to the left of the pub to the Bulls Head and Wheatsheaf in a part of the town known as Old Glossop.

Stage 4
Old Glossop
to Greenfield

Start: Old Glossop (GR SK 041948)
Finish: Greenfield (Dovestone Reservoir) (GR SE 013034)
OS map: Explorer OL 1 Peak District – Dark Peak Area
Distance 9.8 miles/15.8km **Ascent** 1,576ft/480m

View from
Alphin Pike

Paths and terrain: A mix of paths, tracks and lanes, including the Pennine Bridleway's high level route, but with a more adventurous moorland alternative that in places is rough, without signposts and potentially boggy.

What to look out for: There are a number of reservoirs dotted along this stage, including Bottoms, Arnfield, Swineshaw and Dovestone, all originally built to satisfy the need for more water from a growing urban and industrial population. Today the demand is as much for recreation and linking these sites is the Pennine Bridleway National Trail, a 205-mile (330km) route designed principally for horse riders and cyclists, but of course eminently walkable as well, and which runs from Derbyshire all the way to Cumbria.

1 From the centre of Old Glossop walk up the road between the Bulls Head and Wheatsheaf pubs. Continue uphill on Castle Hill. The road becomes a walled track (public footpath) into open countryside. Head for the left hand corner of some trees. Go through a gate with trees on the right and head diagonally left, aiming for the left hand corner of the field at the edge of Swineshaw Reservoir (you have now entered the Peak District National Park). Go through a gap in the wall on the left towards a road.

2 Turn right on to the road and immediately left at Byre House for a footpath. Go past a cemetery and bear right downhill, crossing a stream, then bear left following a wall on the left until you reach a lane. Follow the lane downhill and before it bends to the right take a path on the right, over a stile into paddocks. Cross several more stiles before arriving on Padfield Main Road.

3 From the centre of Padfield, walk down the main road towards Hadfield and cross over the old railway line (now the Longdendale Trail). At the end of the lay-by, just past the trail, take a footpath through an old turnstile and downhill to a track and wall. Turn right along the track for 120m to a gap in the wall. Go through the gap following signs for the Trans Pennine Trail and walk along the edge of Bottoms Reservoir. Cross over at the weir and at the end take a zig zag path up to a lane. Turn right and head uphill to the church on the left, and the busy Woodhead Road.

4 Cross the Woodhead Road and immediately go up a cobbled track ahead to a large ancient cross in 'Stocks' green. At the top turn left and take Arnfield

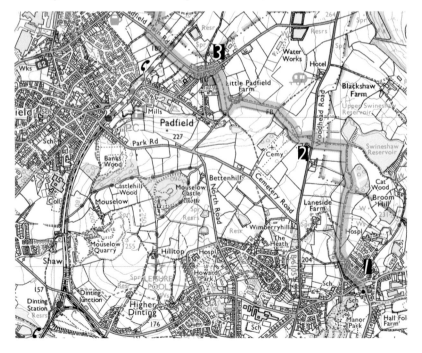

Lane to Arnfield Farm at the end. Follow the lane round in front of the farm buildings out into open countryside and under a line of pylons. When you reach a track go left and follow it down to the footbridge.

From here the main route heads north west towards Mossley on the Pennine Bridleway, but for a more challenging moorland option go to the 'moorland alternative' route described on page 35.

5 Stay on the track (the Pennine Bridleway) and cross between two reservoirs and over the brow of the hill before descending down to a lane. Turn right on this lane and descend to a housing estate.

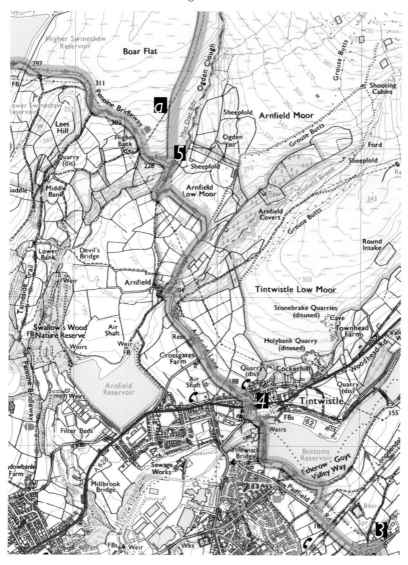

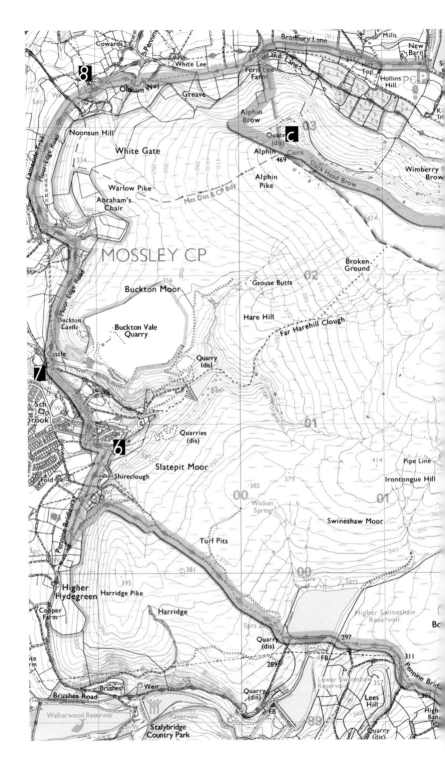

6 Follow the road to the left and continue forwards at the first roundabout. Pass the bowling green on the left and entrance to Stalybridge Country Park on the right and continue forward on Castle Lane towards a quarry. At the entrance of Buckton Vale Quarry take the track up to the quarry and almost immediately turn left on the Pennine Bridleway.

7 Contour round the hill on this track, then pick up signs for the Oldham Way until you arrive at a tarmac road. As the road descends, take a small path on the right signposted 'Oldham Way'. Follow it over a stream and down to a T-junction on a tarmac road, where you should go right (ignore signs to the left).

8 Follow the route for 1km to Fern Lee Farm then go through the farm downhill on a cobbled track. It goes behind a set of mill cottages and arrives at Dovestone Reservoir.

A moorland alternative

At point 5, cross the bridge and walk up through a gate to a Peak & Northern Footpaths Society sign indicating routes (Higher Bank). The path over to Chew Hurdles is not clear but keep Ogden Clough to your right until you reach a well used path at Ogden Brook.

a) *At first there is an obvious route through the heather, with stakes denoting the way ahead. However, the terrain becomes boggy and the path all but disappears. Continue in roughly the same direction until you reach a clear path along the edge. Below, on the other side of the valley, is Chew Road.*

b) *At Chew Hurdles turn left and walk along the ridge with a succession of spectacular views. Head for the trig point at Alphin Pike, beside the rocky shelter.*

c) *From here the route downhill is easily identifiable, but with many paths to choose from take the one which turns sharp right to the lane and along to Fern Lee Farm. Continue on to Dovestone Reservoir.*

Woodhead tunnel

Longdendale: roads, rail and pylons

As you walk from Hayfield to Padfield and Bottoms Reservoir you will traverse three valleys: the Sett Valley, Glossopdale and Longdendale. The last of these is possibly the grandest but bleakest valley in the Peak District, towered over by Bleaklow and Holme Moss and dominated by a chain of enormous pylons which carry the main electricity supply between Yorkshire and Manchester. Other features in Longdendale are the line of five reservoirs which were begun in 1847 and the railway which once linked Manchester and Sheffield. The trackbed is now the route of the Trans Pennine Trail, but the tunnels survive. Despite all these post-industrial additions, Longdendale's haunting beauty makes it still worthy of inclusion in the national park.

The first tunnel was built in 1845. The line cost £200,000 and, because of the horrific conditions and lack of concern for safety, 32 lives. As the tunnel was effectively 'one way' in 1852 a companion tunnel (the Up tunnel) was bored to allow for more trains at busy times. Because both tunnels were narrow, airless and unsuited to steam trains, a third, two track tunnel, was completed in 1954 which carried passenger trains until 1970 and freight trains until the line closed in 1981.

Meanwhile the two Victorian tunnels found a new function when the Central Electricity Generating Board (CEGB), planned to construct the national 'supergrid' and intrude on this wild and remote landscape. Following pressure from the National Park Authority and the Friends of the Peak District to put the cables out of sight, and a public inquiry, they agreed to route three miles of cables through the Up tunnel. By 2007 the condition of these cables was deteriorating so National Grid, the successor to the CEGB, decided to relocate them to the third tunnel.

This destroyed any chance of reopening the railway but relocation went ahead despite objections from the Friends and the National Park Authority.

Beyond the tunnel the pylons march down a further eight miles of Longdendale and the Friends continue to campaign for a complete undergrounding. To that end, and working with the likes of the Campaign for National Parks and the John Muir Trust, the Friends have persuaded National Grid to spend some of the £500 million recently earmarked for undergrounding pylons in national parks and AONBs on improvements along the Trans Pennine Trail at Dunford Bridge.

Today the function of the railway has passed to the A628 road which links Manchester and Sheffield. This single-carriageway road, crossing the Pennines at a height of up to 1310ft (400m), has been condemned as congested and hazardous since the 1960s when plans first surfaced for a Manchester-Sheffield motorway. This scheme (which was vigorously opposed by the National Park Authority and the Friends) was never fully implemented and survives only as a short motorway-grade bypass (the M67) east of Manchester and the Stocksbridge bypass (A616) near Sheffield. However these two 'improvements' had the effect of encouraging more heavy traffic to use the A628 rather than the longer route via the M1 and M62. The resulting pressure on the villages of Tintwistle, Hollingworth and Mottram-in-Longdendale has led to demands for a bypass of these communities from the 1970s onward. Successive governments have approved and then shelved the scheme; the last version failed at public inquiry in 2009.

Friends of the Peak District has for many years campaigned against the proposal for a bypass, fearing it could revive the call for a trans-Pennine motorway. It has been suggested that the impact could be reduced by running the road through a new tunnel, but the Friends do not see this as an answer as it would encourage more traffic which would then be deposited into already congested roads at either end. Instead the Friends advocate weight restrictions on the existing A628 to discourage HGVs, traffic calming in the villages and 'soft measures' to encourage walking and cycling and improve public transport.

John Bull

Woodhead

War memorial obelisk by Pots and Pans Stone

Greenfield (Dovestone Reservoir) to Holme

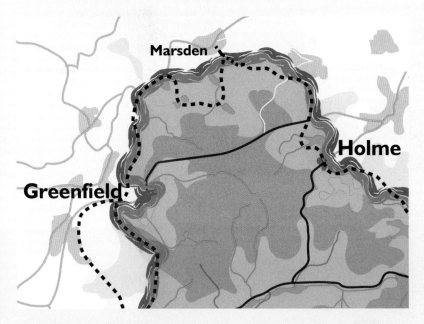

The Boundary Walk now reaches the northernmost edge of the national park, where it climbs up on to the high South Pennine moorland, a bare and open landscape dotted with small reservoirs. Lower down are former mill villages like Diggle, Marsden and Holme, linked by packhorse trails and other ancient routes that criss-cross the hills. From the tops there are terrific views, early on over Saddleworth and Stalybridge towards Manchester; then after crossing the watershed and the historic Lancashire/Yorkshire boundary there are new horizons over Huddersfield and the conurbations of West Yorkshire. The sense of transition is very strong as the bulky moors of the Dark Peak merge into the South Pennines, a solid upland barrier that separates northern England down the middle. Indeed, for the next 200 miles or so it forms a largely continuous body of high ground that stretches all the way to the Scottish border. This northern edge of the national park is a rugged and uncompromising landscape, but with a wild beauty all of its own.

Stage 5
Greenfield
to Marsden

Start: Greenfield (Dovestone Reservoir) (GR SE 013034)
Finish: Marsden (GR SE 049116)

OS map: Explorer OL 1 Peak District – Dark Peak Area & OL 21
South Pennines

Distance: 10.6 miles/17km **Ascent:** 1,959ft/597m

Dovestone Reservoir from Alderman Hill

Paths and terrain: There are plenty of high, sometimes rough
but invigorating moorland paths in this stage, with a few steep
climbs and exposed stretches where care will be needed in
adverse conditions.

What to look out for: Dovestone Reservoir is regarded as the
northern gateway to the national park and is a popular venue for
all sorts of outdoor activities, including sailing and birdwatching.
Walkers and climbers scale the rocky crags that ring the narrow
valley, which are also home to ravens and peregrine falcons. Near
the village of Diggle the historic Standedge canal tunnel (the longest
and deepest in the country) begins its subterranean journey, while
on the moors above is the Pennine Way, Britain's oldest official
long distance path.

1 From Dovestone Reservoir car park entrance at the main road walk downhill and take the first lane (Hollins Lane) on your right. Follow the road around a wide right hand bend, to where it veers left and a driveway joins to your right.

2 Take the grass footpath just inside the driveway uphill, through two fields. Where it meets a driveway track to some properties on your left, continue straight over on a path that continues uphill. The path then meets another track going across it. Cross this track and bear left onto a second path (the Oldham Way). Follow this track uphill to the obelisk (war memorial) near the hilltop outcrop known as Pots and Pans.

3 Behind the obelisk follow a path that leads over the remains of a wall. Turn left at the end of this short path and progress uphill to a gate and stile in the corner of the fencing, and cross the stile. Follow the well-established path in front of you go, up onto a higher ridge and then turn sharp left to follow the path up to an outcrop of rock (Shaw Rocks) and continue onwards.

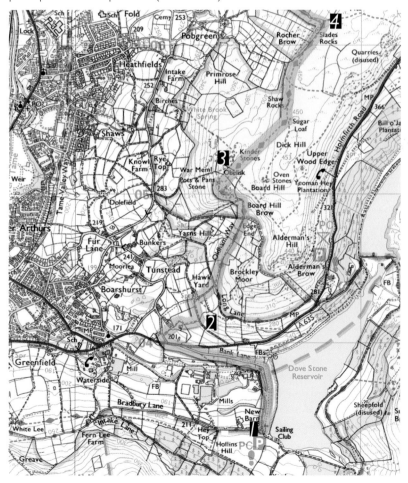

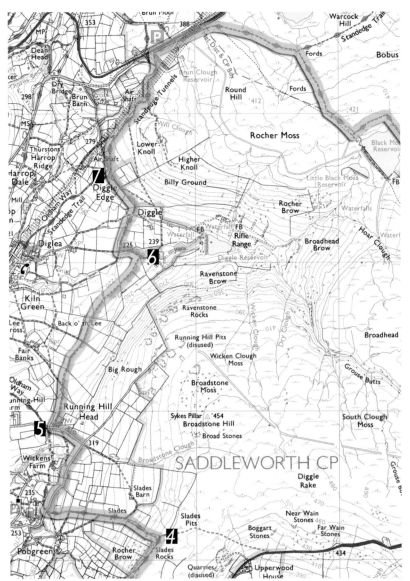

4 Continue along this path with wire fencing on your right, and eventually you will see a stone wall begin on your left. Continue onward to a break in the stone wall where a walled path emerges. Take the enclosed track on the left and follow it for 800m down to the road at Pobgreen. Turn right into the road and continue uphill until the road ahead turns into a track and a lane leads away to your left. Take the lane to your left.

5 Follow the lane downhill, and once rounding a slight left bend, you should see the public footpath fingerpost on the right hand side of the lane, at the

edge of a property. Continue past the property and along a narrow fenced-in path. After a small fenced area leave on the far left, then go immediately right and traverse the field with the field boundary wall on your right. At a stile at the far end switch to the other side of the wall and eventually enter a large expanse of land. Follow the track straight ahead then along a ridge to meet a gate at the far end.

6 Turn left into lane beyond, and once over a bridge take the first right into the lane. Where it turns sharply right take a grass track ahead until a gate at the far end. Go through the gate and bear left to follow an indistinct path along the left boundary to a gate, then via a short track and the front of a property to the road and an elevated gate on your right, with a fingerpost directing to the Pennine Bridleway.

7 Follow the rugged track uphill to Brun Clough Reservoir car park. Take the Pennine Way on the far side of the car park onto Marsden Moor (and from Greater Manchester into West Yorkshire). With Redbrook Reservoir to the left, branch right at a large upright boundary stone. Approaching the next reservoir (Black Moss), go left at the path junction, through an open gateway and down between reservoirs. It continues across an open moor and via Blakely Clough to eventually reach a raised stone platform with a small mast on top.

Marsden from the Colne Valley Circular Walk

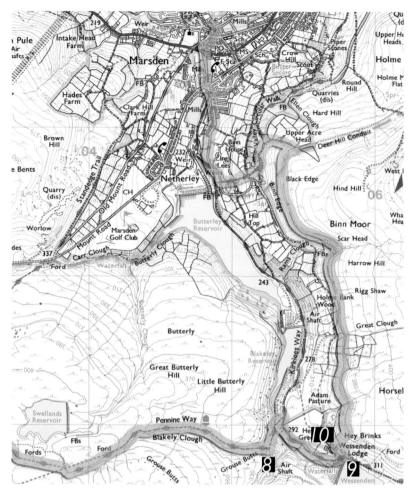

8 Follow the Pennine Way down a steep bank to cross a stream via a plank bridge, then up to a firm track. Turn right and follow this as far as the dam of Wessenden Reservoir.

9 Take a grass path, leftwards, behind the back wall of Wessenden Lodge. Almost immediately turn right (back on yourself) up a track parallel to the Pennine Way until you reach the main path along the edge.

10 Turn left on the path (a designated heritage trail) and alongside a drainage ditch with a raised bank. At the National Trust 'Binn Moor' sign, where the path goes sharp right, take the path to the left down past a house to a lane. Take the second footpath signposted 'Colne Valley Circular Route' down narrow grassy steps, across a farm track, through a gate and down a walled path to the road. Turn right and go straight across at a mini roundabout on to Fall Lane past Marsden football club. Then take the left fork under the bridge, then immediately right alongside the stream to the Riverhead Brewery Tap.

Stage 6
Marsden to Holme

Start: Marsden (GR SE 049116)
Finish: Holme (GR SE 107058)
OS map: Explorer OL 1 Peak District – Dark Peak Area & OL 21 South Pennines
Distance: 8.5 miles/13.7km **Ascent:** 1523ft/464m

Holme Moss in winter

Paths and terrain: A variety of paths and tracks, including well-used bridleways and lanes, as the route follows an undulating course around the national park's north eastern edge.

What to look out for: There are plenty of absorbing sights, many of them further afield, including Emley Moor transmitter, a Grade II listed concrete tower that is one of the tallest freestanding structures in the UK. Looking back into the Dark Peak, the view is dominated by the bulk of Black Hill, the third highest hill in the Peak District at over 1,909ft (582m) above sea level.

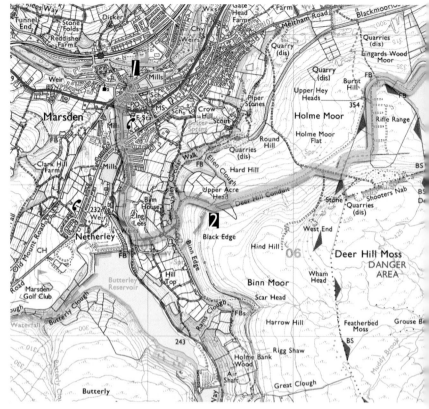

I From the Riverhead Brewery Tap, walk along Argyle Street with the river on your right. Bear left under the tunnel and come out at Marsden football club and bear right. Cross the mini roundabout and go uphill for approximately 1km. When you see the reservoir on the right, take the narrow walled footpath on the left. Go round a house and cross a farm track, up to a lane. Go left uphill, through the National Trust gate and up to the drainage ditch. Turn left and head towards a solitary house on the brow of the hill ahead.

2 Once at the end of the conduit, continue past a house and join the tarmac lane that borders Deer Hill Reservoir, with great views towards Huddersfield and Leeds.

3 Three quarters of the way along this straight lane take steps down the bank on your left as far as the sluice gate that runs alongside, and where a metal handrail on your right comes to an end. Back track around the end of the handrail by way of a tiny earth path leading up a very short bank, which then almost immediately joins a wide flat track.

Route up to the quarry

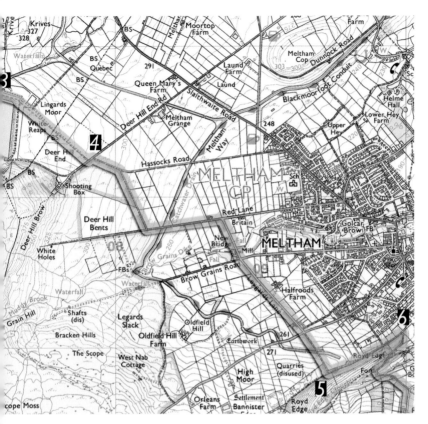

Continue ahead on this track towards a small area enclosed by high green-wire security fencing. Walk alongside the fencing to a stone wall and take the step stile over it. Continue on the wide track straight ahead as it crosses two large fields alongside the left hand boundary, with the village of Meltham in front of you. Exit through the gate ahead, then turn left.

4 Almost immediately take the bridleway on your right. Follow it to the end, keeping to the left edge of the large fields. At the end, turn left onto an unmade road. Proceed along this road until passing a farmhouse on your left, then take the lane on your right. Follow the lane across two junctions and on to an unmade road marked as a public footpath.

5 Shortly after ascending over the brow of the hill as the track bends right, turn sharp left and follow along the steep Royd Edge. The track becomes a tarmac lane and when you reach the first property on your right, turn sharp right immediately afterwards into Hebble Lane. The facilities of Meltham village centre are just a short walk ahead at this point.

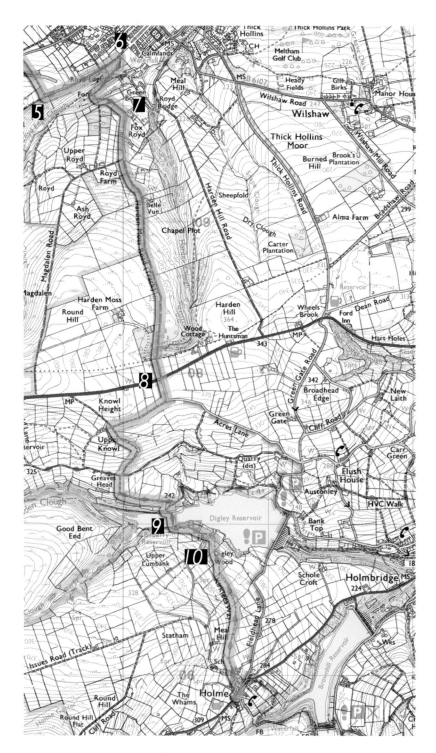

6 Follow the lane down to where it ends in a parking bay. Leave by the metal swing gate straight ahead, and on to a narrow path. Where the low wall on your left finishes turn left along another narrow path and follow it straight on as it crosses over a lively brook by way of a concrete bridge. Follow the path uphill and into a wooded area, where it swings to the left and widens. Follow it out of the woods by way of a much narrower and uneven path.

7 When approaching a metal gate ahead, swing right before reaching it, to walk along a driveway of a property to the end, then turn right onto a tarmac lane. Follow the lane uphill until the lane forks and take the left branch onto an unmade road. As the ascent evens out, merge left on to a drive and proceed to the A635 Holmfirth Road.

8 Cross this main road with care for the lane opposite. Over the brow of the hill, at a sharp left bend, take the track on your right via a stile. Follow it downhill until before a private property turn left into a wide recess in the wall, and through a smaller gate on to a grass track. Follow this downhill until it meets with another, crossing it for another almost opposite (to your right) which leads down to Bilberry Reservoir.

9 Cross the dam between Bilberry and Digley Reservoirs and follow the path around to your left, crossing diagonally through a field to exit in the top corner. At the end of the next field cross a stream/ditch and, immediately afterwards, branch away from this path and walk diagonally up the hill on a faint grass path towards a stone wall.

10 Go through the wall gap and on through fields. It becomes a walled path and leads into the village of Holme. At the end turn left into a lane, then turn right into the centre.

View of Deer Hill Reservoir

Pennine Way across eroded top of Bleaklow

The Pennine Way and access to the hills

High on the bare and windy slopes of the South Pennines, midway between Diggle and Marsden, the Boundary Walk shares a couple of miles with the Pennine Way, a famous old trail whose history reflects our close relationship with this precious upland landscape.

When it opened in 1965, the Pennine Way was the first long distance footpath to be created in Britain, a testing but exhilarating walk from Edale in the Peak District all the way to Kirk Yetholm just across the Scottish Border. But the Pennine Way idea took shape as early as the 1930s and at its heart was the issue of public access to the Peak District moorland. At that time, over 50 square miles of Kinder Scout and Bleaklow were out of bounds and jealously guarded for grouse shooting; it was reckoned to be the largest area of privately owned land in England to which the general public

were completely excluded.

A rising chorus of protest, mostly from the surrounding urban populations, came to a head with the Kinder Scout Mass Trespass in 1932, and through the work of tireless campaigners like GHB Ward, the Clarion Ramblers and Sheffield CPRE's own Phil Barnes. Another was Lancashire-born Tom Stephenson, who dreamt up an idea for a continuous walking route the entire length of the high Pennines. Not only would it be physically and spiritually enriching, he reasoned, but prising out new public access could unleash an unstoppable momentum for change.

The Pennine Way idea captured the popular imagination, but the fight to create it proved long and hard. Despite its designation following the National Parks and Access to the Countryside Act in 1949, persuading reluctant landowners

Old Nags Head, Edale, start of Pennine Way

triumphed and crowds flocked to Edale in search of challenge and adventure; but the harsh terrain and often harsher Pennine weather took its toll - and not just on the unfit and ill-prepared. The fragile peat uplands started to erode into boot-sucking bog and it wasn't long before the Pennine Way became shorthand for drudgery and toil, so that its star waned and its popularity fell away.

Fast forward several decades and much has changed. The Countryside and Rights of Way Act 2000 at last delivered a right of public access to the hills and moors, building on earlier national park access agreements to open up the Peak District's hitherto forbidden moors. The path itself has largely recovered, thanks in part to lines of carefully-placed flagstones recycled from disused Pennine mills. And people continue to walk the Pennine Way, albeit in smaller and more manageable numbers, discovering that this remote upland path that begins its 268-mile journey northwards by crossing Kinder Scout, Bleaklow and Black Hill, offers us moments of solitude and space that are increasingly rare in today's ever more hectic world.

and defiant water authorities to agree a route on the ground took over a decade; and even amid supporters there was disagreement. In 1951, the Sheffield and Peak District branch of the CPRE held a 'Local Pennine Way Conference' at Edale where some speakers registered their unease that a waymarked path could be routed across the middle of Kinder Scout. Might it not compromise the mountain's wild spirit, some asked, or lead novice ramblers into difficulties?

In the end the Pennine Way

Pennine Way at Jacob's Ladder

It's also surely no coincidence that our oldest trail starts in our oldest national park, demonstrating just how much the landscape of the Peak District matters and that connecting with high and wild places, in particular, meets a deep-seated need inside us all. Whether you follow the Pennine Way for a fortnight or just a few minutes, it's ultimately a reminder that the freedom to walk among our own hills that we now take for granted was hard won.

Andrew McCloy

The Church of St Nicholas,
High Bradfield

Holme to Low Bradfield

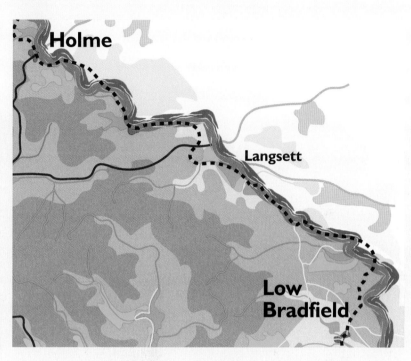

The Boundary Walk now shifts its outlook to the east, into Yorkshire, with large centres of population such as Huddersfield, Bradford and Barnsley a comparatively short distance away. Despite this, Black Hill and endless swathes of rising moorland above Langsett and Ewden seem to form a protective barrier around the national park and there are relatively few routes into this sometimes bleak upland wilderness. The route itself is no less hilly, criss-crossing narrow valleys, many of which were dammed to create small reservoirs and often cloaked in dense plantations of conifers. Amid these foothills there's a string of historic villages and small farming settlements, like Bolsterstone and Bradfield, the latter having the distinction of being one of the largest parishes in England whose reach extends as far west as the Upper Derwent Valley. It's also a reminder that people made a home here long before more recent and widespread urban growth.

Stage 7
Holme to Langsett

Start: Holme (GR SE 107058)
Finish: Langsett (GR SE 211004)
OS map: Explorer OL 1 Peak District – Dark Peak Area
Distance: 10.5 miles/16.9km **Ascent:** 852ft/260m

Langsett Reservoir

Paths and terrain: A mix of moorland paths, bridleways and surfaced lanes. Some of the woodland sections can get a little boggy and take care crossing the A628 approaching Langsett. Between Harden and Winscar there is minimal waymarking.

What to look out for: The route passes a series of small reservoirs, including Winscar which has a sailing club. Beyond is the hamlet of Dunford Bridge and a short section of the popular Trans-Pennine Trail that is open to walkers, cyclists and horse riders. This stretch was formerly a railway line with trains once emerging from the Woodhead tunnel to the west, but now the traffic-free route offers a quieter passage across the northern Peak District.

1 From the bus terminus in the centre of Holme walk through the hamlet, with The Fleece Inn on your left. Just past Holme Castle turn right for the signposted Kirklees Way (KW) down through sloping fields. Cross the Brownhill Reservoir feed via a footbridge, then climb up to overlook Brownhill Reservoir and cross the dam between this and the adjoining Ramsden Reservoir.

2 At the road, turn right and just before the car park continue to follow the KW left, up the hill, alongside a wood. At a bridleway junction (with the KW continuing right) take the Holme Valley Circular (HVC) path ahead up the hill. Shortly, at a point just past the path down to the left, and turning slightly back on yourself, continue right along a well defined path up Crow Hill. This soon re-joins the KW, becoming a rocky road/bridleway called Ramsden Road.

3 At the main road bear left, now off the road and down a rougher route, continuing along the KW until a junction with the HVC, where both turn right continuing past farm buildings and into the conifer plantation. Here the KW continues ahead. Take the first forest road track to the right (the HVC) and follow this clearly defined route that snakes over Reynard Clough. Go past more buildings and eventually emerge at the end of the plantation on to Linshaws Road.

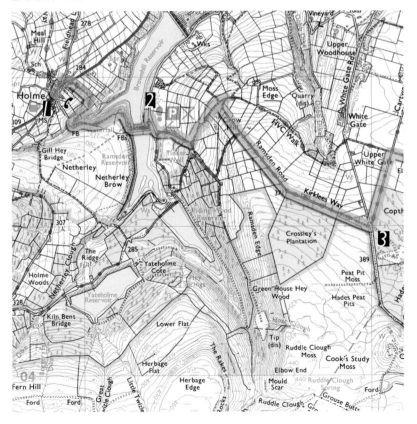

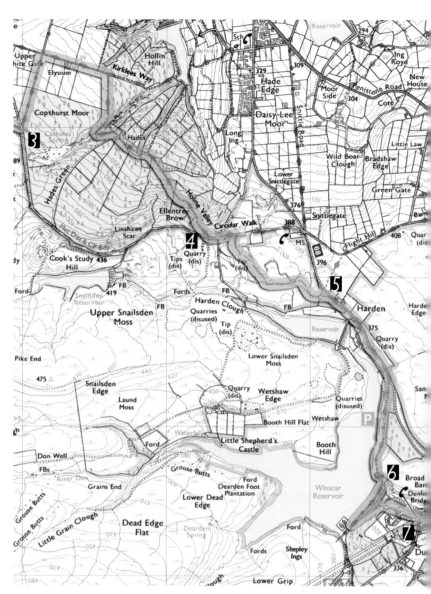

4 Turn left and follow the road around the edge and to the end of the conifer plantation. At the end, just after a private road to the right, follow a bridleway on the right to the road at Harden (this track can be boggy and splits into many routes - keep to the left of the tip of Harden Reservoir and head towards the houses).

5 Continue along the road beside Winscar Reservoir, turning right down to the reservoir car park. Walk through the car park to the far end for a track to the dam overlooking Dunford Bridge.

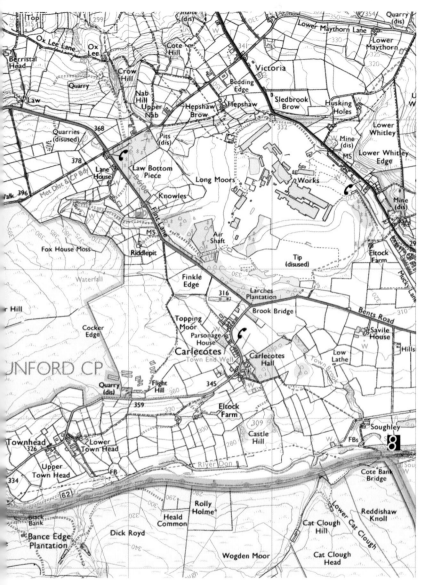

6 Go across the dam and at the end immediately turn sharp left and drop down along the path between the conifer plantation and the dam wall, to arrive in Dunford Bridge.

7 Follow the popular Trans Pennine Trail towards Hazlehead. At Cote Bank Bridge take the path up the embankment on the left and to the bridge.

8 Follow the track across the bridge and over the trail, bending to the left and then through a gate. Follow the path with the wall on your left.

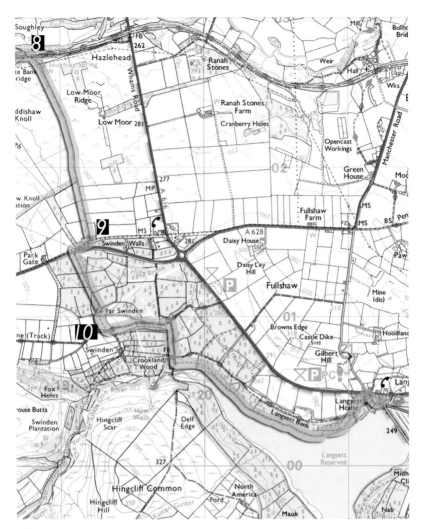

9 The path becomes surfaced as it approaches the houses ahead. At the old Manchester road go right to cross the (new) A628 Woodhead Road (take care - fast traffic) and then ahead, following the signposted footpath straight through the conifer plantation.

10 The path drops down over a stream and at the wall ahead take a left turn to pick up the Barnsley Boundary Walk (BBW), avoiding the immediate footpath on your right. Follow this along the side of the plantation and then into it. At the junction slightly turn back on yourself to continue along the undulating BBW, then turn sharply right on meeting a second track before the tip of Langsett Reservoir. Continue left on the well-used BBW trail through the plantation along the side of the reservoir to emerge towards the dam end of the reservoir at Langsett.

Stage 8
Langsett to Low Bradfield

Start: Langsett (GR SE 211004)
Finish: Low Bradfield (GR SK 263920)
OS map: Explorer OL 1 Peak District – Dark Peak Area
Distance: 10.5 miles/16.9km **Ascent:** 1,346ft/410m

Low Bradfield

Paths and terrain: One or two steep climbs in and out of the narrow valleys, plus plenty of stile-hopping across fields and a little road-walking.

What to look out for: The village of Bolsterstone has its origins in Anglo-Saxon times. St Mary's Church was founded in 1412 and there is a fine Celtic cross in the churchyard. Bradfield also has a long history, but more recently has become known for its brewery and for the legendary 'Côte de Bradfield' hill climb on the 2014 Tour de France - a yellow bike was hung over the door of the Old Horns Inn in its honour.

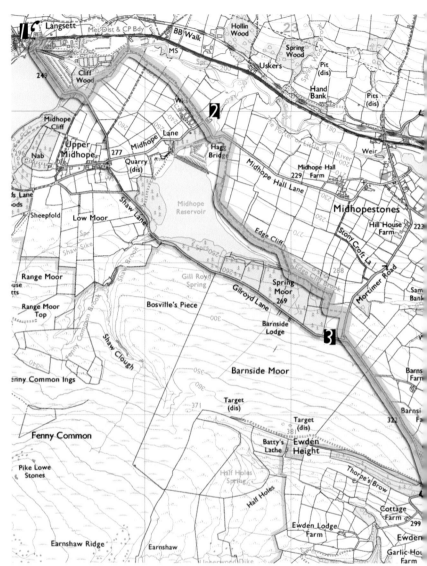

I Leave Langsett Barn car park on the path to the reservoir and turn left to reach the road. Follow this over the dam and just after Cliff Wood take the path on the left down to the Little Don River. Skirt the edge of the wood and then walk through it, shortly coming to a bridge over the river. Don't cross it, but instead carry on along the path through fields, with the river on your left, slightly climbing until you reach the old waterworks at Midhope Lane.

2 Continue directly along the road taking the first path right climbing up into the plantation along the side of Midhope Reservoir. Continue along Edge Cliff, dropping down through the plantation to Edge Cliff Brook and follow this

to the end of the plantation following the path right and then left to reach Mortimer Road. Turn right up the road then left into Gilroyd Lane (take care - there's not much traffic, but what there is can travel fast).

3 Walk along the road past the drive to Barnside Cote Farm, then Wind Hill Lane, both on your left, and just as the road turns back on itself to start a steep descent, take the path immediately ahead. This follows the wall on your left (not immediately obvious at first) and just before the buildings ahead, where three walls meet, take the metal-framed stile before you.

4 Turn right on entering the wood on a path that becomes a track. On passing a house on the right, bear left uphill to reach stone gate posts. Go right to join Heads Lane into Bolsterstone.

5 On entering the village square, just before reaching the church, turn sharp right at the Village Hall and go downhill on Yew Trees Lane. Ignore a turning on the left for Ewden village and continue downhill, going left over a stile for a path down through woods. Join another path at a small bridge over a stream and continue left to a gravelled path, which becomes Pheasant Lane. Turn right at the end, downhill towards Ewden Village.

6 Go straight ahead at the bottom and follow the lane between blue waterworks notices. It curves round the end of More Hall Reservoir and goes over a bridge to become Jack Lane. After 100m go right through a metal gate for a path along the edge of a wood and up to cross a stile through the wall. Continue uphill following the line of the wood, over another stile, and at the third stile turn right onto a broad farm track. Continue on this until just before it meets a road, where you should turn left on the signposted path.

7 Go diagonally left and head for the intersection of two walls and a stile. In the field follow the boundary wall to the left, then the woodland boundary fence to a stile in the

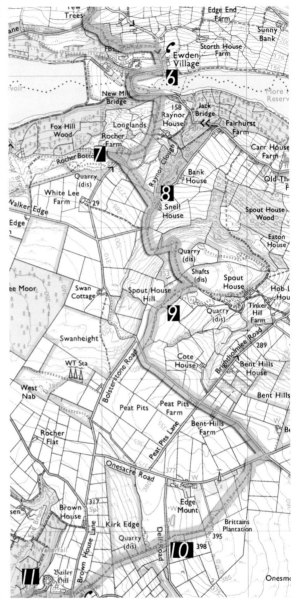

fence. Enter the wood and go steeply downhill, crossing a footbridge over a stream, and climb up the other side on to the road by Snell House.

8 Turn right, up the road, and where it turns sharply right before a bridge cross the stile on the left above the road for a path. Beyond the trees turn diagonally right and climb uphill, heading towards some quarry workings. Turn left on to a broad track and follow this sharply right at the top of the slope. Head

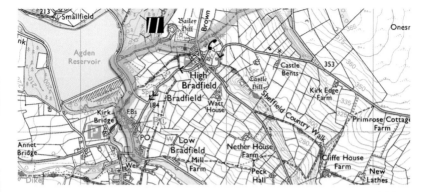

for a large holly tree on the skyline to a dented gate and continue on the farm track, then cross a stile on the right to follow the wall on your left.

9 When you meet a farm track follow this ahead and continue until you reach Bolsterstone Road. Turn left on to the road, go over the first crossroads and at the second turn right towards Edge Mount (signposted Bradfield). After 100m cross a stone stile by some trees on the left. Cross several fence stiles, a fenced track, and via a ladder stile over a wall descend to cross the road.

10 Continue the path downhill through fields to join the road to High Bradfield. Go left to reach the Old Horns Inn and turn right on a cobbled road towards the church.

11 Follow the path alongside the church, head round right up to a path and then left through the burial ground to a gap in the wall, and take the path down to the road around Agden Reservoir. Turn left on the road and, at a house on the right, go through a narrow ginnel. Turn left just before the footbridge to follow the stream. Turn left along the lane to reach Low Bradfield.

Agden Reservoir

Peak District pylons

Landscapes and energy

Anyone walking from Holme to Low Bradfield will notice wind turbines. For some they will gladden the heart, knowing that on a windy day they will be providing vital low carbon energy, powering local homes, farms and industry and helping us avoid the worst impacts of climate change. For others, they are an eyesore, inefficiently culling the wind at the expense of the majestic Pennine landscape and the taxpayer alike. As ever, the truth lies somewhere in between.

Few doubt the requirement to move away from dirty fossil fuels for the sake of reducing the impact of climate change. We clearly need to generate more renewable energy but it must be in a way that is sensitive to our countryside and especially our finest landscapes, such as national parks. Wind alone cannot meet our needs; therefore we need a mix of technologies from hydropower, anaerobic digestion to solar and wind. But it must be located respecting the landscape it sits within.

This is not evident from the views from this section of the Boundary Walk. Looking north and east towards Holmfirth and then Penistone, the eye is drawn first by many isolated small turbines, often providing a crucial new source of income for farmers, increasingly under pressure to diversify. Then looking towards Blackstone Edge and Spicer Hill in the east, much larger turbines – a mishmash of sizes – dominate the horizon. The largest are now out of scale with the patterns of settlement and enclosure in this special Pennine fringe landscape. The original, much smaller windfarm at Royd Moor (installed in the 1990s) is now dwarfed and lost among the modern monsters.

But it is undeniable that Yorkshire is a landscape of power. From the higher moors, like Thurlstone, Langsett and Broomhead, the huge power stations at Ferrybridge and Drax, way to the east, glower and steam like modern dragons.

Fed traditionally by Yorkshire coal, they are now in their last throes of evolution and – for a little while yet – survive on imported coal, gas or biomass. Where our energy comes from next is not readily apparent. And we must also change tack and find ways to use less energy, and more efficiently.

There seem to be two failures here and both relate to planning or, rather, the lack of planning. On a landscape scale, as seen from this part of the walk, an increasingly incoherent planning system has led to an unsightly mix of wind developments and almost no other forms of low carbon development. Where is the hydropower that once powered the mills of the Holme, Don and Loxley valleys? Nationally, why couldn't the current wind capacity be planned more holistically and equitably? Simply put, poor planning is allowing the 'salami-slicing' of the landscape, especially our remoter landscapes, and we are all worse off for it.

But it is not all doom and gloom. Thanks to pressure from Friends of the Peak District, punching above their weight with national peers such as CPRE, CNP and the John Muir Trust, National Grid now have £500 million to remove intrusive energy infrastructure from national parks and AONBs across Britain. One of the first schemes will see the pylons that dominate Dunford Bridge and the nearby Trans Pennine Trail removed, hopefully by 2023. This comes on the back of forcing the predecessor of National Grid (the Central Electricity Generating Board) to route the transmission cables through the Woodhead Tunnels in the 1960s to keep the high moors free of industrial clutter. Clearly none of this is cheap but our finest landscapes are surely worth it.

Andy Tickle

Turbines from the High Peak Trail

Damflask Reservoir

Low Bradfield to Millthorpe

An interesting section full of contrasts, one moment cresting small patches of purple heather moorland and the next plunging down into densely wooded valleys and hopping between in-bye fields. There are more great views from the tops and plenty of interest for naturalists, including Sheffield and Rotherham Wildlife Trust's Wyming Brook nature reserve and the wooded Rivelin valley. It's also a relatively accessible stretch of the Boundary Walk, lending itself to day walks using local public transport, because despite the rural feel Sheffield is only a few miles away - over a third of the city lies within the Peak District National Park. The boundary skirts around the outer urban edge, separated from the core of the Peak District by the open strip of the Eastern Moors and the famous gritstone edge of Stanage.

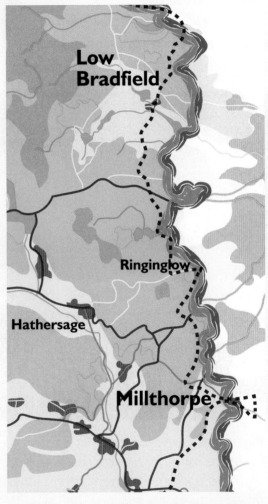

Stage 9
Low Bradfield
to Ringinglow

Start: Low Bradfield (GR SK 263920)
Finish: Ringinglow (GR SK 291837)
OS map: Explorer OL 1 Peak District – Dark Peak Area
Distance: 9 miles/14.5km **Ascent:** 1,508ft/460

Ringinglow Moors

Paths and terrain: Field paths across mostly rough and rolling pasture contrast with woodland rides and moorland tracks, ending high on the Peak District's eastern edge.

What to look out for: Even though the city centre of Sheffield is only a few miles away there are some lovely paths and quiet spots, including Wyming Brook above the Rivelin valley which is a Site of Special Scientific Interest. Bomb craters beside the route just before Ringinglow Road date from the Sheffield blitz in 1940 when German bombers targeted the city's steelworks and heavy industry.

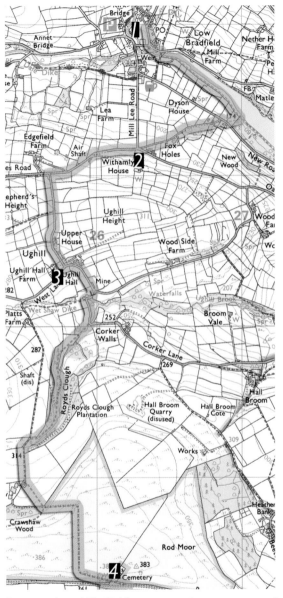

I From Low Bradfield Post Office walk downhill with the cricket ground on the right. Where the road swings right take the road left (Lamb Hill), and then a footpath on the right to cross a bridge. Go left on a path to Damflask Reservoir. After 700m go right, uphill inside the edge of woodland to a road. Turn right and take the byway opposite (signposted Bramble Wood Cottages) which becomes a grassy path and leads to a road junction at the top of Mill Lee Road.

2 Follow the road, signposted Ughill and Strines, rising gently uphill. As you reach the crest of the slope, take the road off left (Ughill Road) and follow it past Upper House on the left to a T-junction.

3 Turn left and go downhill following Tinker Bottom then Corker Lane (signposted Dungworth and Sheffield), soon crossing two streams. Ignore the footpath on the right and at a sharp left bend go right on a footpath immediately before the second bridge. Cross the field close to the fence on the left and through a metal kissing gate. Continue on the footpath, making for a ladder stile into a plantation, where the path goes left. Turn left where the footpath joins a farm track, and bear left just before the house, taking a path across the field to a farm track. Turn left on the track and follow it until you meet a road, with Crawshaw Lodge on the right.

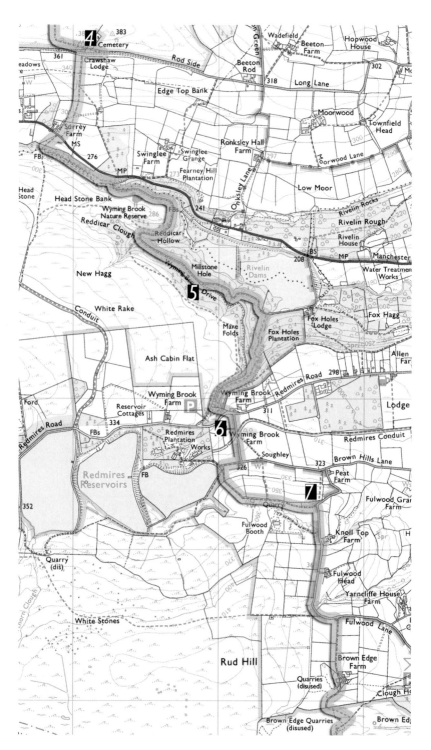

4 Turn right, then left across a broad verge to a footpath sign and stile. Take the path downhill to the main road (A57). Turn right and then cross with care to the footpath going over a stile and down a field (veering slightly away from a wall on the right) to a footbridge over Hollow Meadows Brook. Immediately before the bridge, take the footpath on the left (signposted Rivelin Dams) alongside the river to an unsurfaced road at a stone bridge. Turn right for about 1km (ignoring footpaths on the right) until you reach a large retaining wall, and go left at a fork in the road.

5 Take the road to Rivelin Dams down to a grassy area on the left. Turn right on a path (before the road crosses the stream) and follow the path up steps and through woods, crossing footbridges to an open area with stepping stones on the right. Ignore the stepping stones and take the footpath left (signposted Redmires Road) uphill to a road. Turn left to Soughley Lane.

6 Turn right along the lane and where it bends sharp left take the path to the right. Approaching a metal gate take the path branching left and follow it uphill with a wall on the left. The path broadens and levels out. Just before a metal gate cross a stile to the right and follow footpath signs (via a quarry) to a sunken track. Go left on the track to reach Fulwood Head Road.

7 Turn right on Fulwood Head Road and follow this round a bend to the left. Turn right on a footpath through stone gateposts up the drive to Brown Edge Farm. Beyond the farmyard go ahead through the middle gate and along a walled lane to another metal gate. Cross a stile and take the left of two paths, around the foot of a heathery bank, then up through a gap in the bank for a path to Ringinglow Road. Turn left to finish at the Norfolk Arms pub at Ringinglow.

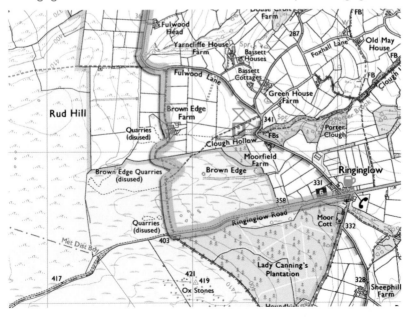

Top of Wyming Brook

Stage 10
Ringinglow to Millthorpe

Start: Ringinglow (GR SK 291837)
Finish: Millthorpe (GR SK 317764)

OS map: Explorer OL 1 Peak District – Dark Peak Area, OL 24 Peak District – White Peak Area

Distance: 9.3 miles/15km **Ascent:** 964ft/294m

Houndkirk Road

Paths and terrain: The first part of this stage is across high, generally open moorland, with good views, then the route descends to the fields and woods below where the ground can be heavier.

What to look out for: Much of the high and exposed moorland bordering Sheffield is managed by the RSPB and the National Trust via the Eastern Moors Partnership, which seeks to balance nature conservation and sustainable land management with public access. There is a network of footpaths and bridleways, as well as large areas of open access, plus internationally renowned climbing crags.

1 From the Norfolk Arms pub on Ringinglow Road, take Sheephill Road opposite before taking the Houndkirk Road bridleway on your right. Continue along Houndkirk Road for approximately 2.5km then just before some small crags on the right, there's a footpath sign on the right. Opposite this, on your left, is an unsigned and indistinct path, grassy at first, that heads straight east. Cross the low point of a small ridge and continue downhill to a wooden gate into Hathersage Road (A625) opposite Whitelow Lane.

2 Carefully cross over the main road to the pavement on the far side and turn right. Walk alongside the road past the millstone on a plinth (a Peak District National Park boundary marker) and shortly after take the bridleway on the left downhill into woods. Ignore the bridleway going off to the right and instead continue down to flatter ground and cross a wooden bridge to reach a path junction. Turn left to pass through stone gateposts, then immediately turn right to cross a stream on stepping stones.

3 Continue on the track uphill, ignoring side paths, to reach a path junction with two benches on the right. Turn right uphill, keeping on the main track, and immediately after a gate turn left on to a path with a wall on the left. Go down to a footbridge and cross a stream.

Smeekley Wood

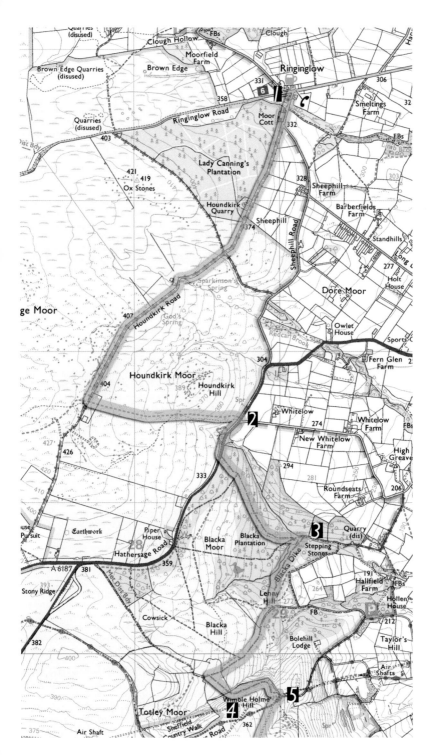

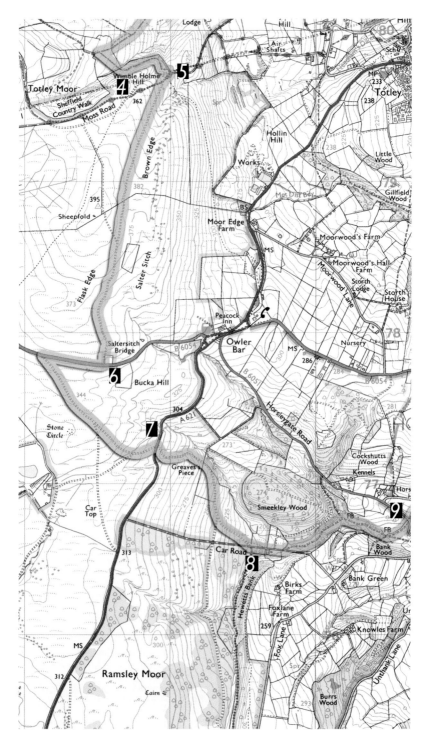

4 Go through a gate, turn left on a gently rising path which bends to the right, and through a gate to a substantial stony track called Moss Road.

5 Turn right and take the lesser track branching left uphill through the heather (do not take the first track on the left). Continue on a grassy track up and over the hill for 2km, passing a large cairn on the hill to the left, eventually to reach a gate and main road (B6054).

6 Cross the road and turn right to walk on the roadside verge for 400m, then go through a gate down to the left on to a broad track that curves gently away from the road over rough grassland. Ignoring cross paths, go down to a tarmac track, then go left and over a cattle grid to the main road (A621).

7 Cross the road and stile beside a metal gate to a grassy track going right and downhill. Continue through a pair of substantial stone gateposts and then gently downhill before levelling out with a fence on the left, to pass through a wooden gate into Car Road (bridleway).

8 Turn left down Car Road to pass Smeekley Farm on the right, and where the road begins to rise go left (next to a metal gate) to take the broad path with a stream on the left. After crossing a stream on a stone bridge pass through a large gate and turn immediately left on a path going up the field to meet a road.

9 Cross the road to take a signposted path slightly to the left, between fences, going uphill to meet a minor road at Blacksmiths Cottage. Turn right on to the road and go uphill.

10 Continue on the road for 1km. When it bends sharp right, take the footpath (restricted byway) on the right. Follow this down to the road. Turn right on the road and down into Millthorpe.

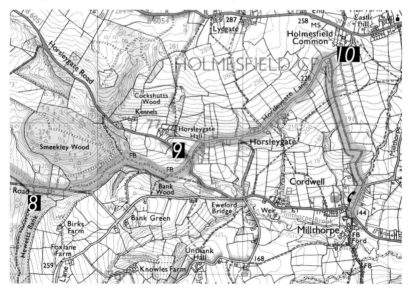

Blacka Moor, looking down on Totley

Sheffield's beautiful frame

'Protecting the Beautiful Frame' is the title of Melvyn Jones' history of Friends of the Peak District (and the CPRE Peak District & South Yorkshire branch). It may seem like a strange title, but Ruskin once described Sheffield as a 'dirty picture in a golden frame'. Certain viewpoints on the hills above Sheffield – the stretch of the Boundary Walk from Rivelin Dams, up Wyming Brook Drive and onwards to Ringinglow – offer some of the best places to understand the 'beautiful frame'.

The setting of the city of Sheffield in the basin of the five river valleys means that, once you get up into the hills, you can appreciate huge panoramas stretching almost further than you think it's possible to see with the naked eye. Unless, of course, you've picked a day when the clouds have rolled down and smothered it all; if so, bad luck. You can see a big, industrial city completely encircled by open landscapes – Sheffield framed by hills.

This is an important aspect of why the green belt is so important to Sheffield, and why CPRE is proud of the pivotal role of Gerald and Ethel Haythornthwaite in securing that green belt, almost 15 years before the Peak District National Park was designated. Containing the sprawl of the city suburbs up the river valleys into the Peak District meant that there was, and still is, a sudden, dramatic edge between city and country. It's a jagged edge, because the countryside reaches deep into town along the river valleys, principally where old mills and forges have long since been abandoned and the rivers themselves, once the toxic dumping grounds for factory waste, have been reclaimed as green corridors.

The landscape to the west of Sheffield is also home to over a dozen reservoirs, some built to supply industries and others for clean drinking water. Reservoirs are unsubtle, man-made

Misty Burbage

the green belt contains the city; the national park protects what is within its boundaries.

As a result, the narrow stretch of green belt land between Damflask and Stannington, between Wyming Brook and Fulwood, between Ringinglow and Whirlow, between Owler Bar and Totley, is a nervous and constantly threatened fringe landscape. It's where the countryside begins in earnest for many Sheffield people, yet it's also under development pressures that would be unimaginable one mile to the west, once you cross into the national park. Some of the sites that developers are most keen to cherry-pick for lucrative housing are in the very places where CPRE fought for - and won - as the places where the city ends, and its beautiful frame begins. As Sheffield embarks on a new Local Plan, the edges of that frame are being chipped away once again.

Andrew Wood

interventions in the landscape, and yet Sheffield has taken them to its heart as places of tranquillity and recreation. It is a landscape that has worked hard, supplying water, power, minerals, building materials and food for centuries, and the city of Sheffield could not have thrived without it.

It is a pity, in many ways, that the national park boundary was not drawn to coincide with the green belt boundary. If that had happened, then the beautiful frame - the idea that the landscape can fulfill a truly special function, at a national scale, even when it is touching right against the edge of the city - could have been enshrined in policy. We know in practice that it does have that function, as when anyone extols the virtues of Sheffield as a city, the proximity of the landscape is usually top of their list. For most people the western Sheffield green belt is indistinguishable from the national park, yet in the land-use planning system they are very different creatures:

Fox Hagg above Rivelin Valley

EL
OCT 21
1905

*Nelson's Monument
on Birchen Edge*

Millthorpe to Winster

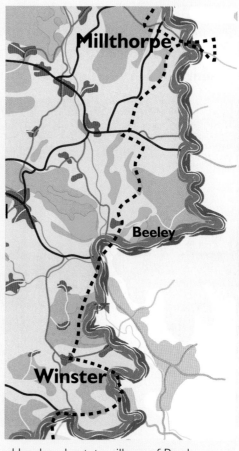

The section begins by climbing on to the high gritstone moors of the eastern Peak District, visiting some notable rocky outcrops along the way. An elegant stone monument on Birchen Edge commemorates Lord Nelson and his victory at the Battle of Trafalgar in 1805. The route then drops down to cross the lush Derwent Valley to finish amid the gentle limestone landscape of the White Peak, with its characteristic stone barns and walled fields. On the way you pass Chatsworth, one of the finest stately homes in Britain, with its elegant parkland and estate village of Beeley. Unusually for the Boundary Walk two of the Peak District's principal rivers are met in quick succession, the Wye and Derwent, which come together at Rowsley. After the heather interlude of Stanton Moor, with its stone circle and huge sandstone boulders, the countryside once again softens, as the rolling dales take over in a more intimate landscape of farmland, scattered woodlands and small villages.

Millthorpe to Beeley

Start: Millthorpe (GR SK 317764)
Finish: Beeley (GR SK 264674)
OS map: OL 24 Peak District – White Peak Area
Distance: 10.6 miles/17km **Ascent:** 1,121ft/342m

Cross in Shillito Wood

Paths and terrain: Firm moorland tracks and some potentially boggy woodland paths. There are a few road sections and crossings, so take appropriate care.

What to look out for: There is an ancient cross in Shillito Wood worth seeking out, plus an historic guide stoop at the nearby path/road junction. Leash Fen is thought to be the site of a sunken village, now a nature reserve that is being allowed to return to a natural mire. Nelson's Monument on Birchen Edge is accompanied by his three 'ships', large rock formations with their names carved on - Victory, Defiance and Royal Soverin (sic).

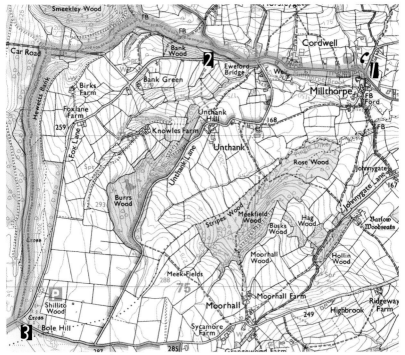

1 This section starts near the Royal Oak pub, where there is a small parking area at the bottom of Millthorpe Lane, close to the junction with Cordwell Lane (B6051). From the junction walk along Cordwell Lane in a westerly direction past the Royal Oak. There is a pavement to start with, but this peters out close to the village, so take care on the busy road. Ignore the two roads to the left, to Unthank and Shillito, and continue along Cordwell Lane until a footpath is reached on the left, next to a small layby, signposted to Fox Lane Top.

2 Follow the footpath through pasture and then woodland for 1km to reach a tarmac lane, ignoring all minor paths to the left and passing the foot of Smeekley Wood. Turn right on the lane for 250m past farm buildings, then take the path (bridleway) on the left. Follow this gently rising path for almost 2km to reach Shillito Wood and emerge at a road junction.

Royal Oak pub at Millthorpe

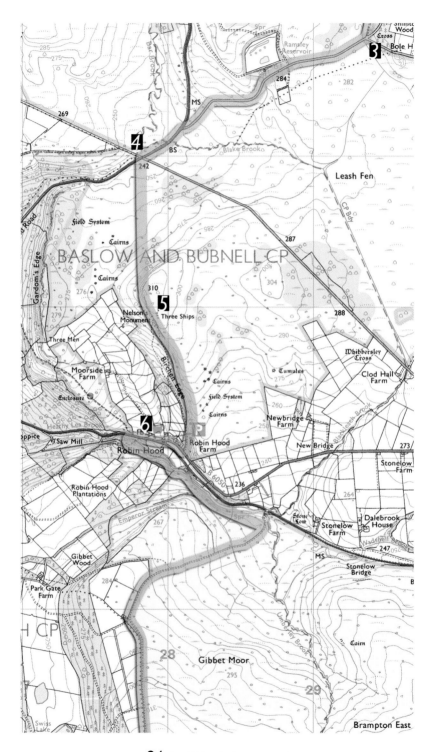

3 Turn right and walk along the road until the A621 is reached. Turn left and walk along the verge as far as a crossroads. This is a very busy, fast road and care needs to be taken here.

4 Go through a gate on the minor road onto open moorland and follow the main path south towards the end of the ridge. After 500m pass two boulders, then look for a faint path on the left which climbs up on to Birchen Edge. At the top turn right on a clear path to the trig point. Continue to Nelson's Monument and his 'Three Ships'.

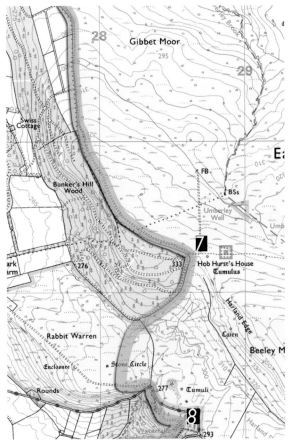

5 The meandering path continues along the top of the edge before dropping steeply to the main track below. Turn left, then right on to the road to reach the Robin Hood pub and road junction.

6 Walk down the busy A619 for 400m, then cross with care for an inconspicuous stile in the fence opposite. Descend the steps, cross over the stream and continue up to a junction. Turn sharp left on to a grass track signposted Hob Hurst's House. The waymarked path first wanders through the valley, then climbs up the hillside to meet a stony track. Turn right on this for 3km and when the woods on the right end, take a quick detour: continue to the Bronze Age barrow of Hobs Hurst's House.

7 Go back to the woods and take the small path which follows the wall downhill to a gate at the bottom. Cross a bridge and fork left on a little path south across the moor to a stony track. Turn left and cross a high stile. Cross the stony road and go through a stile into Hell Bank Plantation.

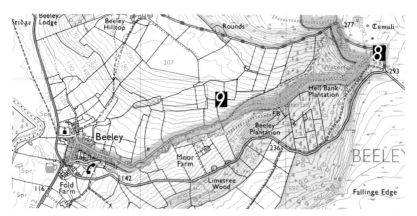

8 Follow the path to cross over a stream and up to a junction. Turn right downhill, and right again at the next junction. The path descends through the woodland valley, re-crossing the stream via stepping stones and emerging through a gate on to a stony track.

9 Continue down to join a tarmac lane which leads into Beeley. Turn left at the end, down to the Devonshire Arms, and the junction with the B6012.

Beeley

Stage 12
Beeley to Winster

Start: Beeley (GR SK 264674)
Finish: Winster (GR SK 242606)
OS map: OL 24 Peak District – White Peak Area
Distance: 6 miles/9.6km **Ascent:** 1,198ft/365m

The Corkstone on Stanton Moor

Paths and terrain: Mostly firm tracks and woodland paths into and out of the Derwent valley, finishing with field paths and an historic miners' route into Winster.

What to look out for: Rowsley is a busy village, featuring two pubs and a working flour mill with tearoom and craft shops. Half of the village is within the national park and it is in fact the national park's lowest point (in terms of height!). The small expanse of heather and silver birch that makes up Stanton Moor is rich in prehistoric remains, including a stone circle and numerous barrows and tumuli.

1 From the centre of Beeley, by the junction near the B6012, facing the Devonshire Arms front door walk left along the road, with a stream on your right to a sharp bend. Turn right across a stone footbridge, through a gate and up across two fields to a minor road. Go through the gate opposite and continue in the same direction. At a signposted footpath junction turn left uphill, to the right of the hedge, then diagonally right up to Smeltingmill Wood, with good views back to Chatsworth Park.

2 Once inside the wood take the right fork and follow the path along the contour until you reach a track. Turn left uphill, between two tall stone abutments (remnants of the disused Burntwood Quarry) and soon turn right on a wide path. Go down to a bridge and on to join a farm road, ignoring paths to the right. Turn right to reach a minor road. Turn left then right on a narrow path leading down to the A6 at Rowsley.

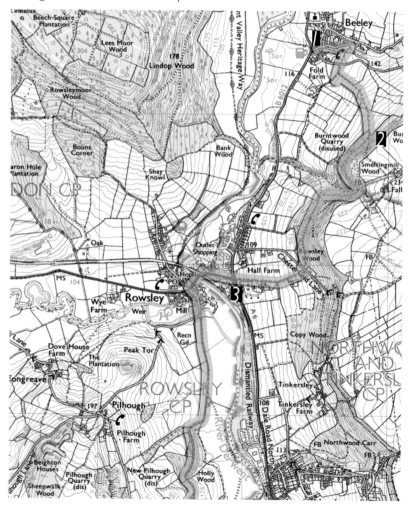

3 Go across the junction with Chatsworth Road and walk ahead along the pavement of the A6 into Rowsley, past the Grouse and Claret pub and over the River Derwent, to a pedestrian crossing. Cross here and immediately turn left along School Lane, past the entrance to Caudwell's Mill car park and over the River Wye to a right hand bend. Continue straight ahead on the tarmac lane for 1.5km to Stanton Woodhouse.

4 At the farm, the track zigzags through farm buildings to a gate. Continue uphill on a wide grassy path and follow this all the way until you emerge on to a minor road.

5 Turn right on the road for 100m and then sharp left on a wide path through an old quarry. It bends round to the right and later doubles back to the left, continuing gradually uphill just inside the wood. Go through the first gate on the right, marked 'Access Land', on to Stanton Moor. Take the grassy path left to join a sandy track and continue ahead to reach Nine Ladies Stone Circle (an interpretation board shows a rather imaginative picture of a religious ceremony).

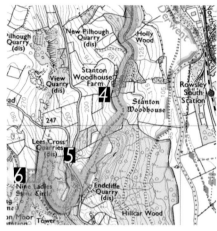

River Wye at Rowsley

6 Continue on the same path across Stanton Moor, with fine views of the Derwent valley to the left, and later Winster on the distant hillside ahead. Eventually you descend to a lane. Turn right and shortly left on a path down to Barn Farm and campsite. Follow the signpost for Winster. The two pubs of Birchover are a short walk away to the west.

7 Continue south towards Winster across fields, following the field boundary and crossing a green lane. The path turns right to descend through Stoop Wood and steeply down to a stile. Follow the path as it drops down into the valley and then climbs into Winster (the remnants of paving are old leadminers' tracks). The path emerges on to the main road near the old Market House in the centre of the village.

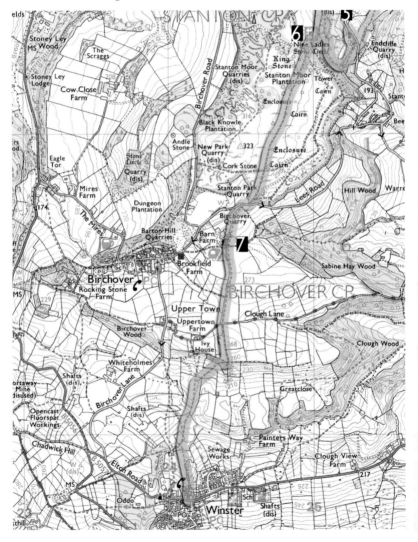

Earl Grey (or Reform) Tower,
Stanton Moor

Line of shooting butts on Bamford Moor

Land management old and new

The Peak District National Park was born in 1951, the same year as the Festival of Britain. The latter was intended as a post-war morale boost to the country, a celebration of industry, science and the arts. The former enshrined the protection - and celebration - of a set of beautiful landscapes. The decade after World War Two was one in which the country expressed its gratitude to its people for their bravery and sacrifice, and a huge and wonderful park, a green heart for the dirty, industrial North, was a grand gesture towards promoting wellbeing.

It's crucial to remember, though, that the national park doesn't just promote wellbeing through recreation and access to nature. Its landscapes supply us with clean water and food, and are taking on increasing significance for how we respond to climate change; managed well, the uplands offer carbon sinks and

a huge shock absorber for the extremes and uncertainties that a changing climate brings, particularly droughts and floods. Of course, the land and the people who managed it were doing this in one way or another long before the national park existed. That raises questions about how the national park has shaped land management, and how it may need to evolve, to change with the times.

Seventy percent of the national park is privately owned, much of it within large estates such as Chatsworth; with the remainder shared between water authorities, the National Trust and the National Park Authority. The day-to-day management of the land falls partly to estate managers, but also to tenant farmers, gamekeepers, conservation groups, not to mention contractors and sub-contractors. Do they have a shared sense of what they're trying, collectively, to achieve for the national park? Almost certainly not.

Let's take a specific, if possibly controversial, example. There is an emerging tension between traditional forms of land management that pre-date the national park by generations, including sheep farming and grouse shooting; and proponents of 'rewilding', who suggest that allowing areas of land and soils to convert to a more natural, less managed state will provide big benefits, not least in terms of resilience to climate change. The reality is that both those approaches have winners and losers. Some birds, such as the golden plover, thrive on moorlands that are managed for grouse, while others, like the whinchat, don't. The same is true economically, and culturally: you can ask a sheep farmer to keep less stock, to set fields aside for non-farming, and you can provide cash incentives to do so. But a sheep farmer may not want to be a 'non-sheep' farmer, and land management for upland storage of storm water is a different discipline requiring different skills and expertise. So any financial or policy intervention will change not only the appearance of the landscape, but the way it functions and what we expect of the landowners and land managers.

At present, huge uncertainties hang over farming as the UK heads for the uncharted territory of leaving the European Union. What will leaving the Common Agricultural Policy entail, and what, if anything, will replace EU legislation on biodiversity and water? On the one hand, agriculture that is less driven by strategic subsidies may be more sensitive to its locality, and we may see a further flourishing of small-scale, locally-branded produce. On the other hand, a push for new international trade deals might sideline UK farming altogether, and derelict, unmanaged farm landscapes may result.

The really interesting question for the future, as we walk along the Peak District boundary, is what will differ about how land is managed, depending on whether it falls inside or outside the national park. The answer is likely to lie in how comprehensively decision-makers can understand the many functions the Park fulfills, and whether the landowners, land managers and other stakeholders can buy into a shared sense of purpose.

Andrew Wood

Walkers and sheep in Chatsworth

Parwich

Winster to Thorpe

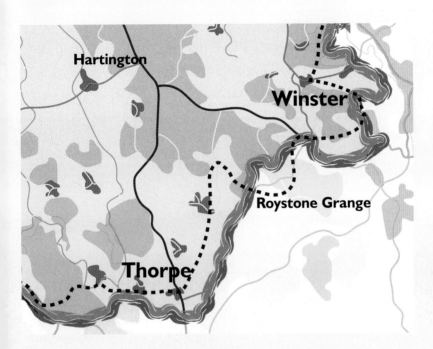

From a start amid undulating and shallow leafy dales to an expansive limestone plateau, this section of the Boundary Walk traces the south east corner of the national park across the open landscapes of the White Peak. There are some fine panoramas and long distance views, and although this is ostensibly a farming landscape it also bears the marks of industry past and present, from lead mining over previous centuries to modern quarrying. A number of recently-erected wind turbines along the ridge overlooking Carsington Water are also very evident. Numerous archaeological sites show that the area has been settled since Neolithic times, with the mysterious tree-covered hilltop of Minninglow certainly worth a visit. Despite its stirring scenery, this is a surprisingly little-visited part of the national park and you are unlikely to encounter crowds of people. Stretches of the Boundary Walk follow the Limestone Way, a long distance walk from Castleton in Derbyshire to Rocester in Staffordshire.

Stage 13
Winster to Roystone Grange

Start: Winster (GR SK 242606)
Finish: Roystone Grange (GR SK 200566)
OS map: OL 24 Peak District – White Peak Area
Distance: 10 miles/16km **Ascent:** 1,083ft/330m

Roystone Grange from the High Peak Trail

Paths and terrain: : Plenty of short grassy field paths, via squeeze stile and gates, usually easy underfoot but intermittently signposted, plus a long stretch of the semi-surfaced High Peak Trail.

What to look out for: Lead ore occurs across much of the limestone plateau of the Peak District and has been mined since at least Roman times. Although the industry is long gone, its legacy can be seen in numerous fields in the shape of small pits, spoil heaps and capped shafts; and villages like Winster and Bonsall are closely associated with it. Much older still is Minninglow, a distinctive tree-topped hill containing several Neolithic burial chambers (concessionary access on foot).

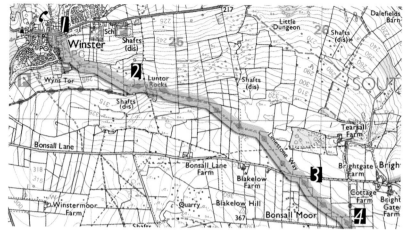

I From Winster Market Hall go up East Bank road to an easily-missed footpath immediately beyond the Old Bowling Green pub. Turn left in front of a cottage, along a tarmac lane and go through the stile behind a small bungalow (East View) on the right. Head up diagonally left through fields, eventually joining a path above fields hummocky from old lead mine working. Keep going up and at a footpath sign beyond a marooned squeeze stile join the Limestone Way.

2 Pass through the next field, below Luntor Rocks, and go through the gate in the top right hand corner. Go through a stile/gate in the wall on your right, then continue with the wall on your left. Continue through fields until the path bends right and up to cross a stile. Go across a field corner and three more fields, then diagonally through a long field to reach Bonsall Lane.

3 Turn left along the road and take the footpath on the right, signposted the Limestone Way. Follow it diagonally across fields and over broken-down walls, through a gate onto a lane. Go left and then immediately right at its junction with Blakemere Lane.

Minninglow

4 After 30m take the gate on the left and go diagonally right to a stile. Follow the path across more fields, bearing left to a walled path. Go left and then, at a path junction, right across several fields. Beyond a stone barn go through the stile in the far right hand corner. Ignore the Limestone Way's obvious route ahead towards a house and go further left (allotments on your left) to the gate stile in the far left corner of the field. Continue down the next, go through the left wall stile, and on beside the wall to a gate in the corner by a small copse and down to a road.

5 Go right along the road, bending left downhill past Abel Lane and into the centre of Bonsall. Beyond the splendid market cross go down Yeoman Street to the junction with The Dale on the right, by the Fountain Tearooms.

6 Take the walled footpath opposite the tearooms and go uphill where, at the top, you turn right in front of the gap in the wall ahead and go through the gate in the corner, under trees. After a gateway, go diagonally right to cross more fields under power lines to a stile with a marker post. Take the path across small fields to a road.

7 Go left along the road, down past Slaley Farm, then up right through the hamlet of Slaley. After this the road bends right and left. Take the second footpath on the right, going diagonally ahead to a gated stile. Cross more fields to a 5-way path junction at a stile, then beyond go diagonally left across the first of several rakes (narrow mined gullies). Take a left fork on a path past old mine workings that is ablaze with wild flowers in season. Go left round a large hole to a double gate.

8 Go diagonally left and then right of a restored barn to a gate in the wall, crossing the next field to Bonsallmoor Lane. Cross the road and follow the Limestone Way along the left hand edge of several fields past Leys Farm. At the end of the field carry straight on along the right hand edge, with Whitecliffe Farm to the left. In the dip of the next field, go through the stile/gate on the right, then left uphill with the fence on your left. Where the fence ends, keep straight on uphill to another stile and the path to a road.

9 Go right along the road, through the hamlet of Ible and downhill to a road junction. Turn sharp left along to Grangemill. Cross the A5012, take the bridleway signposted Brassington and the Limestone Way, and follow it across three fields up to a gateway in the far corner.

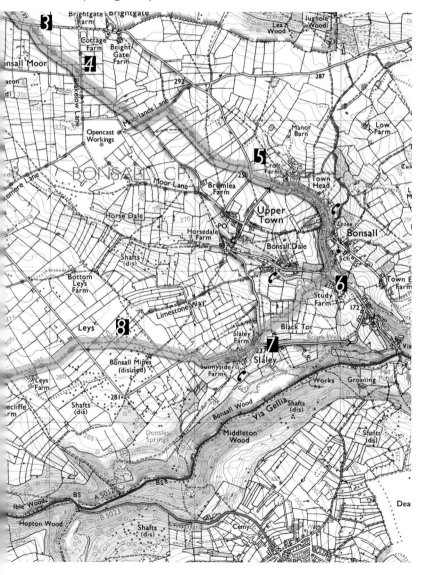

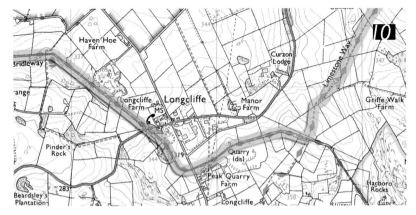

_10_ Cross four more fields on a well-marked path to stiles which lead onto the High Peak Trail. Go right along the trail for over 3.2km of easy walking (also popular with cyclists) until a low hill topped by a clump of trees called Minninglow.

_11_ As you reach a small wood on the left of the trail, almost opposite Minninglow, go through a gate on the right and down to a path that crosses beneath the trail. Beyond the bridge, follow the track down, ignoring the gate in the far corner and instead go through the gateway to its right. Further down the next field take the wall step stile on the left and go downhill on a track. Ahead to the left is a 19th-century pump house and to the right Roystone Grange farm. Go through a gate squeeze, half left across a small field, and through the stile onto a lane.

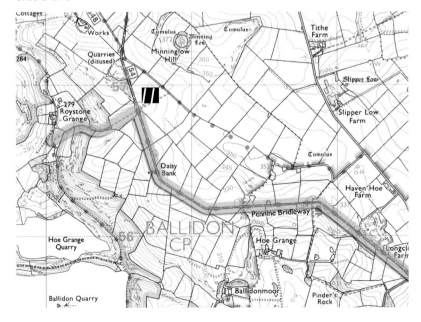

Stage 14
RoyStone Grange
to Thorpe

Start: Roystone Grange (GR SK 200566)
Finish: Thorpe (GR SK 155505)
OS map: OL 24 Peak District – White Peak Area
Distance: 7.7 miles/12.4km **Ascent:** 567ft/173m

Fenny Bentley Church

Paths and terrain: The limestone plateau gives way to gently rolling valleys, via small fields and farms. It can get quite boggy underfoot following wet weather.

What to look out for: Archaeological investigations have shown that Roystone Grange, a remote valley site at the start of this section, has been settled for at least 1,800 years, including 300 years during Roman times. Later, in the Middle Ages, there was a monastic grange (a sheep farm) which belonged to the Cistercian Garendon Abbey, near Loughborough. Further on, Bentley Old Hall at Fenny Bentley (now called Cherry Orchard Farm) has an unusual defensive tower dating from the 15th century and the remains of a medieval moat.

1 Walk down the lane from Roystone Grange farm past the pump house towards Ballidon. Go on past the huge limestone quarries of Ballidon and Hoe Grange. Where you join a road at a hairpin bend, take the right fork downhill and continue past quarry buildings and roads on your right.

2 At Ballidon Quarry's main entrance, by the roundabout with a small quarry wagon on it, turn right onto a tarmac footpath going slightly uphill behind a metal railing, towards the quarry's reception and offices. Turn left onto a path through trees and into a field. Go up the field's right hand edge and through the stile in the top right hand corner. Continue uphill with a fence on your right. At the end of the fence keep straight on to a stone wall corner and go through the stile. Go diagonally across the field to a tall wooden footpath sign, and through the stile onto a road at a T-junction.

3 Cross the road and take the narrow tree-lined Monsdale Lane directly ahead, past a stone barn on the left. Follow it down into the attractive village of Parwich.

4 Where the road joins from the village on the right, go ahead and down to a T-junction. Go right, cross the road, and take the footpath left, parallel to the road to cross a footbridge and gate. Continue with a small stream on your left, go through another gate and ahead to a stile. Beyond this turn right along a track and where it finishes continue on a footpath between hedges to a gate. Cross two fields, keeping left except to avoid boggy patches, and go through another gate and the lower end of Sitterlow Farm yard.

Roystone Grange pump house

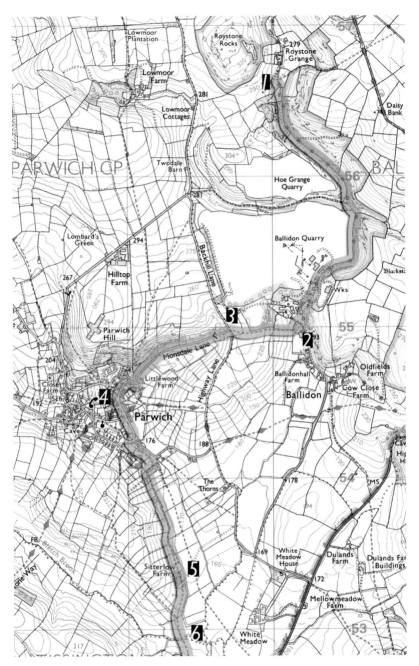

5 Beyond the farm the gated track curves right. Fork left across the field to a gate in the far corner. Continue ahead to a signpost and go through the gate behind it. In the far right corner ahead, cross the footbridge over the Bletch Brook.

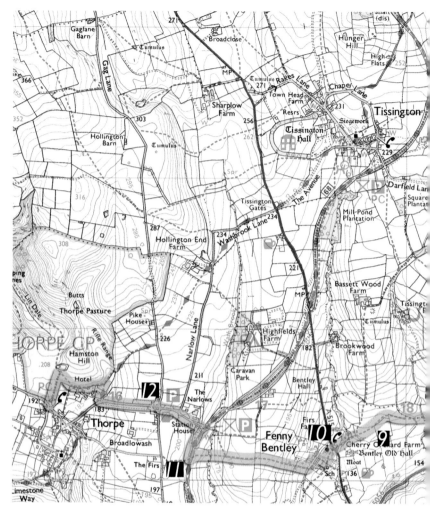

6 Now go uphill to the right of two trees and to a small gate in a fence, with Gorsehill Farm to the left. Go up the hill and down the other side to a stile in the middle of the hedge. Follow the path through fairly new woodland to a stile in the top right hand corner, cross another field and via a gate go diagonally left across the minor road to the end of Lea Cottage Farm track and down through the farmyard.

7 Approaching Lea Hall, go right up the track to Woodeaves and Fenny Bentley, then just after the second cattle grid take the left fork and continue on the track before descending right to a gate stile at the bottom right hand corner of Cloughriddins wood (crossing the grass to a gate into the wood). Go through to another gate and cross the stream. Go half left uphill through fields, then drop down to a gate and a footbridge across another stream.

8 Slant left to go through the farmyard of Woodeaves Farm and then walk down the farm road. Just before the end of the second field take the signposted footpath right to a small gate (up to the right). About 120m on go left, through the wall, and cross the stile to the left of Lees Farm. Cross the farm track and the next two fields. Cross the stream then keep near the right of the field, and go through the metal gateway into the field ahead.

9 Follow the hedge on your left, then aim for the spire of Fenny Bentley church. To the left of the nearest buildings, join a track which leads down to the A515 at the Old School.

10 Cross the A515, then turn right and go through St Edmunds churchyard. On the far side turn left along the lane and after the last house turn right at a narrow metal gate up a footpath. Continue across several sheep pastures, cross Wash Brook via a footbridge to climb up to the Tissington Trail.

11 Go right on the trail until the former Thorpe station, which has a car park and picnic tables but no other facilities. Leave it along the road at the far end, joining another road (Narlow Lane) at a corner. Go ahead past a car park to the Old Dog pub.

12 Take the road to the right of the pub and all the way down to the Peveril of the Peak Hotel. At the hotel gateway go right at the finger post and follow the path through the hotel grounds, then a small field. At the stile turn left and along the wall at the rear of the hotel, keeping to the fence until you reach a stony track at the wall corner. Turn left on this to reach the car park and toilets.

Walking group in front of Thorpe Cloud

Ballidon Quarry, near Parwich in the White Peak

Rock: geology and quarrying

The Peak District's beautiful varied scenery results from two main underlying rock types. The central and southern area is an undulating plateau of limestone, known as the White Peak from the rock's pale colour, and mainly covered by grassland used for grazing cattle and sheep. The limestone was laid down from the shells of marine animals 350-310 million years ago in the Carboniferous period, when the area was near the equator and covered by a shallow tropical sea. Subsequent erosion has created its steep sided valleys ('dales') and striking gorges.

The contrasting wide expanses of heather moorland and peat which cover the northern half of the Peak District, and extend down the White Peak's eastern and western sides, are known as the Dark Peak. It lies on millstone grit: sandstones and shales formed later than the White Peak, from the mud and silt of enormous river deltas. It is higher than the White Peak, reaching 2,087ft (636m) at Kinder Scout, and erosion has led to prominent gritstone escarpments ('edges') popular with rock climbers.

The Peak District's rocks and associated minerals have long been used by man. You can't go far, especially in the White Peak, without seeing the impact of mining and quarrying – both inside the national park and beyond its boundary, which excluded some of the biggest quarries near Buxton.

Minerals exploited in the past included copper and Blue John (a form of fluorspar), but lead dominated for centuries. It was mined extensively in the White Peak from Roman times. The last mine closed in 1939 and the grassed-over spoil heaps and remains of old mine buildings now add interest to the landscape, and remind us of the area's long industrial history. Quarrying is a different, continuing story.

Both limestone and millstone grit

were originally quarried for local building stone, including for the characteristic drystone field walls. Limestone was burnt on an increasing scale to produce lime for agriculture and, as its name suggests, millstone grit was also quarried, often from the edges, to make millstones. Most old quarries were small and have gradually become hidden by woodland. By contrast, modern machinery makes quarrying possible on a huge scale, with inevitable scarring of the landscape, heavy lorry traffic and noise pollution, all of which conflict with the national park's purpose of conserving and enhancing the area's natural beauty.

The National Park Authority has the difficult task of balancing landscape protection with both the national need for limestone and the local need for jobs – its duty is to foster the economic and social well-being of local communities. Most of today's quarries were well established before the national park was created in 1951, as was the UK's largest cement works at Hope, which dominates local views in the Hope Valley. Demand for limestone for aggregates, cement and the chemical industry has continued to increase, and most old mineral planning permissions had no requirements for backfilling or landscaping. However, the Authority has had some success in reducing the number of quarries and preventing old ones re-opening, with the help of recent changes in the law to bring old mineral permissions under modern planning controls.

Some of these legal changes resulted from pressure by the Friends of the Peak District and the Campaign for National Parks. Minimising quarrying's damaging impact is one of the Friends' major campaigns: it opposes new large scale development but supports small scale quarrying for stone needed for local buildings. Long-running and ultimately successful campaigns, working alongside local people, have prevented renewed quarrying on Stanton Moor, and further damage from illegal quarrying on Longstone Edge. However, quarrying remains a threat to the Peak District landscape so continued campaigning will be needed.

John Temple

Climbers taking advantage of an old quarry at Millstone Edge above Hathersage

Ilam Hall Youth Hostel

Thorpe to Tittesworth Reservoir

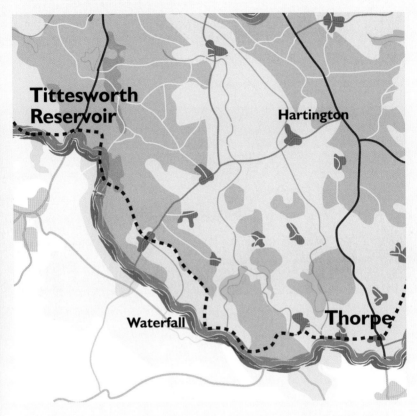

This varied and beautiful section begins with three fine White Peak river valleys - the Dove, Manifold and Hamps. The latter two are unusual in having stretches where the water disappears into fissures in the limestone, often leaving the river bed dry, and re-emerging some miles downstream. Although the route passes within a mile of the Dovedale stepping stones, you are unlikely to meet many people, except at Ilam. Beyond the village of Waterfall the geology changes and you climb on to the high and open Staffordshire Moorlands. The whale-back ridge of the Morridge offers fine views and a real sense of remoteness, as well as forming the south western boundary of the national park.

Stage 15

Thorpe to Waterfall

Start: Thorpe (GR SK 155505)
Finish: Waterfall (GR SK 080515)
OS map: OL 24 Peak District – White Peak Area
Distance: 8 miles/12.9km **Ascent:** 1,086ft/331m

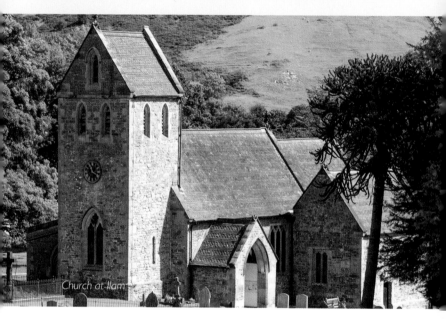
Church at Ilam

Paths and terrain: A steady climb out of the Manifold Valley and a similar descent into the Hamps Valley.

What to look out for: The tall monument by the bridge in Ilam is in memory of Mary Watts Russell, wife of the wealthy manufacturer Jesse Watts Russell who once owned the Ilam estate, and is based on the 'Eleanor crosses' built in the reign of Edward I. Watts rebuilt the hall in the 1820s, as well as the ornate cottages and village school in the Picturesque style. To avoid demolition in the 1930s, the building and much of the estate was given to the National Trust by the McDougall flour family for the public to enjoy, with the caveat that the hall be used as a youth hostel.

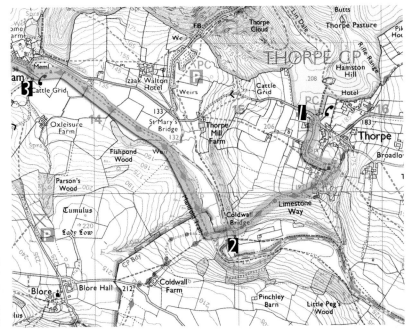

1 From the small car park on the Thorpe-Ilam road, cross the road and walk along Digmire Lane until you reach St Leonard's Church. From here continue along the lane, bearing right and after about 250m go through a gate where the lane becomes a track. Turn right and descend to Coldwall Bridge (part of the old Turnpike route to Cheadle and The Potteries) on the Limestone Way.

2 Cross the bridge (from Derbyshire into Staffordshire) and turn right on the footpath. Contour above the River Dove on your right, eventually dropping to the riverside. Follow the riverside path to reach the bridge at Ilam.

Hazleton Clump near Musden Low

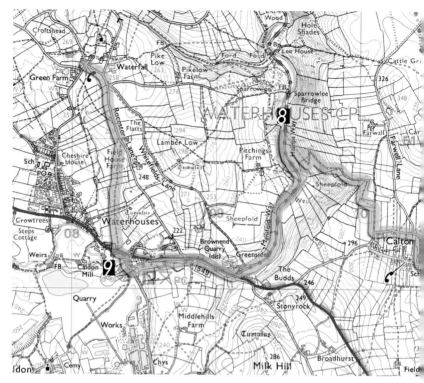

3 Cross the bridge and go past the monument. Continue in front of the row of cottages to enter the grounds of Ilam Hall via a white metal gate to the left of the main entrance. Follow the path past the church to the hall (well worth exploring). Turn left in front of the hall, cross the grass, descend steps and turn right. Follow the path behind the hall (known as Paradise Walk) with the river on your left for 800m, then go through the gate and left over the footbridge.

4 Cross two fields, heading for a gate stile in the wall at the tree line. Go straight up the steep hillside and near the top bear left to the wall ahead and follow it left to a gate. Continue with the wall on your right until you reach a corner in the wall, turn right and follow it to the entrance of Upper Musden Farm.

5 Continue ahead with the farm boundary on your right, and at its end go through a gateway and turn left to follow a footpath alongside the wall uphill. Beyond the next stile go diagonally right over the flank of Musden Low with lovely views up the Manifold valley to distant Axe Edge.

6 In the direction of the cement works (the tall outline of the buildings is a useful directional guide) cross Musden Low, crossing a stile and following the wall in order to descend to a shallow valley. Here turn right, alongside the wall

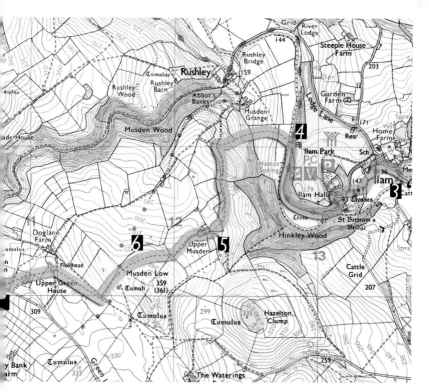

to reach a gate in the corner. Turn left on to a lane and after 100m take the gate on the right (just past Fieldhead Farm) and through fields to a minor road.

7 Turn right on to the road and go over the crossroads to reach the village of Calton. Follow the road into the quiet village. Turn right on the footpath opposite the school, then left on the road for 300m, and at a sharp left hand bend turn right on to a track. After 200m take a footpath on the left, through a small black gate, and follow the path as it zig-zags diagonally down the steep slope to reach the Manifold Track in the valley bottom.

8 Turn left on the track (the trackbed of the old Leek and Manifold Light Railway) and continue to the main A523 road. Turn right towards Waterhouses, cross the busy road with great care, and follow the cycle path which rises away from the road to the car park.

9 Go through the car park and turn right on the minor road and continue to the junction with the A523, with Ye Olde Crown Hotel on the corner. Cross the main road, turn left and after 100m, opposite Bridge House, go through a gate stile on the right into a field. Follow the path northwards through a succession of stiles and fields, rising steadily to meet Rocester Lane. Turn left and continue on this quiet road. Follow the lane for about 600m (ignoring two junctions going off to the right) to reach the hamlet of Waterfall by a phone box.

Ilam Cross

Stage 16
Waterfall to Tittesworth Reservoir

Start: Waterfall (GR SK 080515)
Finish: Tittesworth Reservoir (GR SJ 993601)
OS map: OL 24 Peak District – White Peak Area
Distance: 11.4 miles/18.3km **Ascent:** 1,094ft /333m

Tittesworth Reservoir to the Roaches

Paths and terrain: There are some sections of road-walking, albeit on open moorland with good verges, and one or two potentially muddy farmyards.

What to look out for: As you climb higher on to the Staffordshire Moorlands the views get steadily more expansive. From the broad ridge of the Morridge you can look down to the town of Leek in the valley below, and beyond to the conical shape of the Wrekin almost 40 miles away. Tittesworth Reservoir and the Roaches are also prominent landmarks.

1 From Waterfall take the lane behind the phone box and go ahead across the field. Pass the village church on your right (not into the churchyard) and go through the gate ahead/left, and diagonally down through the field to a footbridge for the lane at Back o' th' Brook. Turn left on the lane and after about 150m take the track which forks right past Gibgreen and Lawnfield.

2 Follow the track bearing right and down to a pond. Across the stream turn immediately left, go slightly uphill and over a stile in the fence corner up to the right. Turn left across three fields, with the stream down on your left, then descend and re-cross the stream at a ford. Go ahead up the spur between two streams to Felthouse Farm. Turn left just before the farm to the lane.

3 Turn right on the lane for 150m then take the next track going off left. Near the foot of the hill before the buildings, turn right through a gate and follow the Hamps Way around farm buildings and across riverside meadows to the hamlet of Ford.

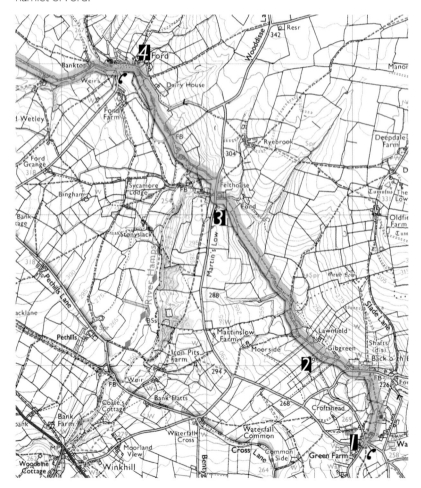

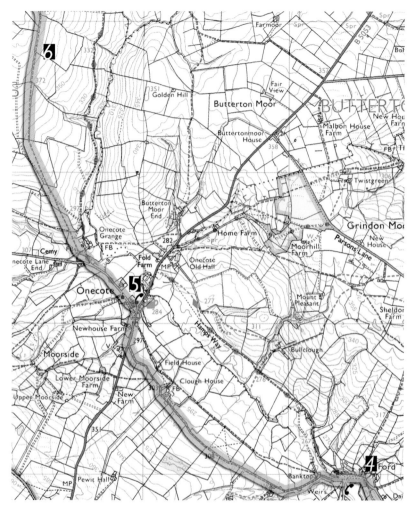

4 Go left on the minor road, left over the bridge and immediately right on Wetley Lane to Banktop. Keep on the road in front of Banktop, which becomes a stony track. Where it turns left keep ahead on a grass track and at Clough House Farm stay on the track to the road. Turn right at the road (B5053) and then left at the next junction into Douse Lane and Onecote village hall.

5 Walk along Douse Lane to St Luke's Church and continue for 300m, then turn right down towards Onecote Grange. Cross the stream over the bridge and pass through the farmyard, to the left of the farm buildings, and up the field to a stile in the top left corner. Continue diagonally left across further fields and follow a farm track to a waymarked stile. Carry on across the field to a stile near a gate and stone trough. Keep the wall on your right up the next field to the top, then on your left through two more.

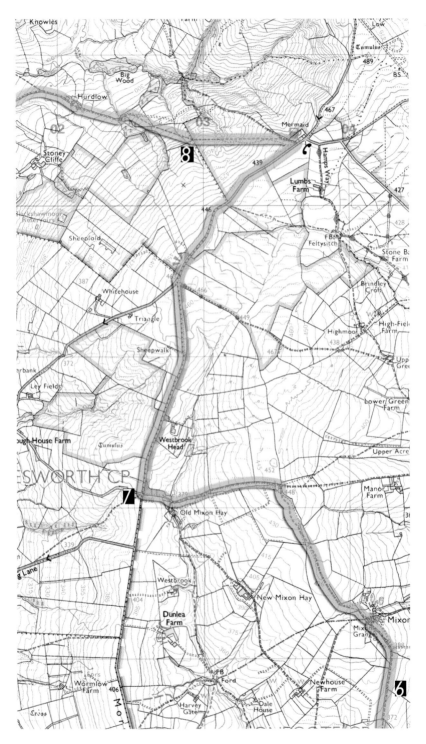

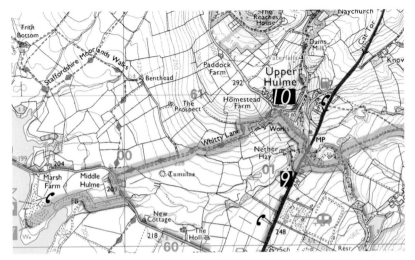

6 At a crossroads of tracks at the top bear left along the wall to a stile. Pass through a short enclosed section and ahead across a field. As you reach Mixon Grange cross a small enclosure to the left of the main buildings, past an attractive Peak & Northern Footpath Society sign, then go half left uphill to join a tarmac track which becomes grassy. At the top, just before the fenced reservoir, turn right to a stile and onto a wide track. Turn left along the lane down past Old Mixon Hay and up to the road (the Morridge).

7 Turn right and follow the road (the national park boundary) for 1.5km to a junction. Bear right and walk along the verge (there's a toposcope after 100m) and continue for 1.1km to just before the old Mermaid Inn (now holiday accommodation). Go left through a gate and bear left – almost due west (double back sharply) to the left of the grassy track and to a sign to Hurdlow. Follow a series of waymarked posts across open moorland, descending to a stile.

8 Drop down to a grassy track and turn left to cross the head of a gully. Cross two fields following waymarked posts and turn left on a stony track (with a copse on your left). Pass through Hurdlow Farm and down to the A53. Shortly before the road, turn right through double gates on a path down to the road.

9 Cross the road very carefully and go right, then after 30m (where the road crosses the River Churnet) left down some steps. Follow the path by a stream, over a footbridge, up fields and through a gate into Upper Hulme.

10 Turn left on the road, then left again on a path around a field and through a gate at the bottom. Continue on a concrete farm track, then left at a footpath sign and right at the next (Whitty Lane). Follow the path and then a stony track to the road at Middle Hulme. Turn left, then right at the former car park on a footpath alongside the River Churnet. After 200m bear right to join the main track to reach Tittesworth Reservoir Visitor Centre and car park.

Dovedale

A tale of two valleys

Dismayed that extensive tree felling was causing irreparable damage to his beloved Dovedale, Frederick Holmes avowed to campaign to save it for future generations to enjoy.

As local secretary for the fledgling National Trust, Holmes galvanised support for his ambition. Throughout the 1930s, hundreds of acres of countryside in and around the Dove valley were gifted to the National Trust by generous benefactors. A major contributor was Sir Robert McDougall (of flour fame) whose gifts include the magnificent Ilam Hall. It was not just individuals, either, as Holmes successfully cajoled Imperial Chemical Industries (ICI) to gift Iron Tors Dale (the missing link between Milldale and Wolfscote Dale) to the National Trust - the first ever land gift by a major commercial donor.

Contemporary travel writers at the time were quick to recognise what was happening. "Dovedale from Hartington to Ilam seems likely to become a national park without a penny grant or help from the government," wrote William T. Palmer in his book *Odd Corners in Derbyshire*. A 1931 government inquiry had recommended the introduction of a National Park Authority for Dovedale, but despite several representations in Parliament to make Dovedale the first national park, no action was taken.

Writing in 1939, Frederick C. Mutton observed, "In the Dovedale area… the nucleus of a National Park has been established." He also acknowledged the work of the CPRE, with the Sheffield and Peak District branch being particularly active. For the first time, voluntary countryside wardens were introduced (a precursor to the National Park Ranger Service?) "…to patrol at busy holiday times and try to prevent visitors leaving litter, uprooting wild plants or doing damage to property - duties requiring much tact." It's a sentiment that still holds true today!

The 1945 *Dower Report on National*

Parks included a map suggesting possible boundaries, with "The Peak District and Dovedale" (as it was then called) providing the blueprint for what would become Britain's first national park in 1951. At last, success for Dovedale, a jewel in the Peak District crown!

Meanwhile, Dovedale's sister – the Manifold Valley - has had a somewhat different tale to tell; yet it adds another fascinating dimension for the visitor. More accessible than the Dove, the lower Manifold has seen lead and copper mining define its history since the Bronze Age. However, its boom time was in the 18th century (quite literally, being the first mines to use explosives underground!).

Owned by the Duke of Devonshire, Ecton copper mines created immense wealth in the 1700s, much of which was used to fund the stunning architecture of Buxton's Crescent in the 1780s. Today, exploration of the old mines, which are now under the stewardship of the Ecton Mine Educational Trust, reveal a dramatic history.

In 1904 the Leek and Manifold Light Railway was built (allegedly amidst rumours that the mines were to reopen). Running just 8.25 miles (13.3km) from Hulme End to Waterhouses (but with 10 station halts) it gained much popularity with tourists travelling in primrose yellow coaches. A boon to the dairy industry and linking with London trains, it carried up to 300 churns of milk daily, and also the famous local Stilton cheeses. Although doomed to close in 1934, an enlightened Staffordshire County Council acquired the trackbed in 1937 and a footpath was laid at a cost of £6,000 (a huge sum in those days). Thus, the Manifold Way was born, described by Frederick C. Mutton as "a pedestrian track – the only one of its kind in the Kingdom". Originally cyclists were not allowed on it and walkers complained that the path was too well made! Nowadays, the Manifold is one of several immensely popular resurrected trackbeds in the Peak District.

Ever evolving, two splendid, contrasting valleys with stories to tell as you pass through on your Peak District circumnavigation.

Paul Keetley

Manifold Valley near Ecton

Shutlingsloe - a hill sometimes called the 'Cheshire Matterhorn' as seen from the Roaches

Tittesworth Reservoir to Bollington

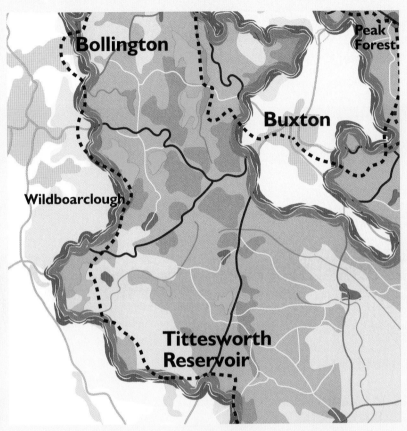

The Boundary Walk now swings round to the western edge of the national park, from Staffordshire into East Cheshire, and along the way it features some notable peaks and ridges. Shutlingsloe, Tegg's Nose and the Saddle of Kerridge above Bollington are among the highlights, each giving sweeping panoramas but also involving some sharp ups and downs. Tucked away at their foot you cross infant rivers like the beautiful Dane and the Bollin at Langley. Macclesfield Forest and Tegg's Nose are popular outdoor destinations for mountain bikers and horse riders, as well as walkers, and there's a good network of paths and bridleways which are likely to be busy at weekends.

Stage 17
Tittesworth Reservoir to Wildboarclough

Start: Tittesworth Reservoir (GR SJ 993601)
Finish: Wildboarclough (GR SJ 982685)
OS map: OL 24 Peak District – White Peak Area
Distance: 10.1 miles/16.2km **Ascent:** 1,174ft/358m

The Roaches from the Morridge

Paths and terrain: Mostly undulating field paths, some not always obvious, and some rough slopes. There's a little road-walking along lanes, so be careful of traffic.

What to look out for: From Meerbrook there are great views across to the Roaches, a gritstone escarpment almost two miles long which defines the south-western edge of the national park. The name Roaches has evolved recently from 'Roches' and is the French word for rocks. It used to belong to the Swythamley Estate but was purchased in the 1980s by the Peak District National Park Authority. Today Staffordshire Wildlife Trust has taken on the day to day management of the beauty spot.

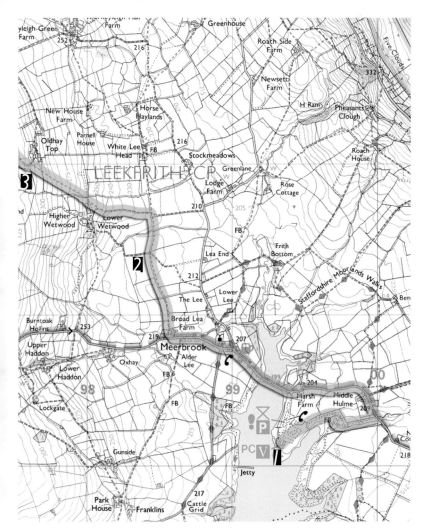

1 Leave the visitor centre and turn left along the road to cross the bridge over the end of the reservoir. Follow the road through Meerbrook and past the Lazy Trout pub and St Matthews Church. Go through Broad Lee Farm to a stile and path beyond, initially with a hedgerow on the left. Cross several fields until you reach a track.

2 Cross the track and continue forwards, across a stream, then go left at a crossroads of tracks towards Lower Wetwood Farm. Before the farm buildings take a waymarked footpath signposted Oldhay Top. About 50m after the last farm building go up a steep field, take the waymarked path through the hedgerow and cross the stream. Via a stile cross a footbridge, then head uphill towards the farm buildings at Old Hay. There is no path but there are footpath signs. Go through two more stiles to reach the farm track.

3 Turn left on the waymarked track uphill and then right (at the driveway entrance to New Zealand). Follow the road from New Zealand until it goes sharply left. Take the footpath on the right by a gate. Cross the stile by the gate on to a wide stony path, quite overgrown in places, to Gun End Farm and a road.

4 Turn left on to the road for about 500m. (Walk in single file on this road, as there is no pavement and cars travel quite fast round the bend.) Where the road curves sharply to the left, take the farm track on the right signposted Hawksley Farm.

5 After 100m turn right on a track downhill until you reach Hollin Hall. Just before the entrance to the hall take a path on the left. Go over a stile and follow the re-directed path around Hollin Hall to rejoin the track and go immediately right, over a stile and across a field, down to Gig Hall. At the bottom of steep steps turn right on to a grassed lawn and across a metal bridge.

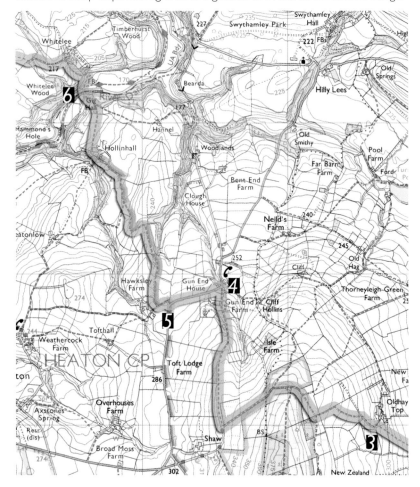

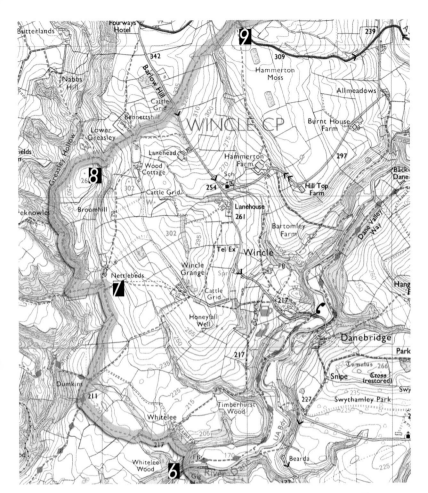

6 Follow the signposted footpath by the fence to go round Whitelee Farm, reaching a stile and a track outside the farm entrance. Turn left and follow this to a gate, then go over a stile and two fields to meet the signposted Gritstone Trail. Turn right, then at the next junction bear slightly left and head towards Nettlebeds Farm.

7 Just short of Nettlebeds Farm turn left at a path junction and steeply down to a signpost. Turn right to reach a wooden footbridge. Cross this and follow the valley, passing a further footbridge and stiles. At Lower Greasley Farm bear right and uphill out of the wooded valley.

8 At a farm driveway turn right and follow the stony track up to the road at the entrance to Bennetts Hill Farm. Turn left and follow the road up to a junction. Cross the road (Barlow Hill) and stile, continue on the indistinct route across fields and gently downhill to the left edge of a wood, then up to the Wild Boar Inn on the A54 road.

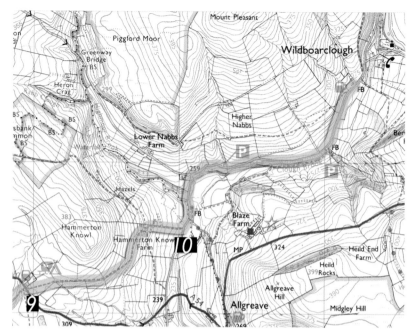

9 Cross the stile to the right of the pub and over a field with more stiles towards Hammerton Knowl Farm, keeping the large mound of Hammerton Knowl on the left. Pick up the vehicle track and head left for Hammerton Knowl Farm. Turn right and go over the stile, through a gate and follow the driveway downhill to meet an unclassified tarmac road.

10 Follow this undulating road for 2km along the Clough Brook Valley to the Crag Inn near Wildboarclough. Stay on the right side of the road not only for safety reasons, but also for good views of Clough Brook as you walk in.

Tittesworth Reservoir Visitor Centre

Stage 18
Wildboarclough
to Bollington

Start: Wildboarclough (GR SJ 982685)
Finish: Bollington (GR SJ 937778)
OS map: OL 24 Peak District – White Peak Area
Distance: 8.5 miles/13.7km **Ascent:** 1,532ft/467m

Old quarrying machinery on Tegg's Nose

Paths and terrain: There is a little light scrambling to reach the top of Shutlingsloe, but nothing very serious, otherwise it's a mix of forest tracks and field paths, with a few sharp slopes.

What to look out for: Plenty of interest on this absorbing stage, beginning with Shutlingsloe - a hill sometimes called the 'Cheshire Matterhorn' because of its almost conical shape and which gives spectacular views of Axe Edge, the Roaches and even Jodrell Bank Radio Telescope. Macclesfield Forest and its associated reservoirs are well known for both nature conservation and recreation, while Tegg's Nose is a former hilltop quarry that's a now popular country park and has a visitor centre with plenty of local information.

1 Keep the Crag Inn to your left and continue on the unclassified tarmac road for 100m, then bear left onto a steep surfaced track and follow it over a cattle grid. Follow the sign to the left of Shutlingsloe Farm. (Be sure to look at the crafted bracelets made by the children of the farm, for sale at the pathway honesty box!) Follow the path to the summit of Shutlingsloe. Continue up this prominent path to the trig point and toposcope on the slight ridge.

2 With Macclesfield Forest visible to the north, descend a very steep stone flagged path which gradually flattens out. Turn left through the metal kissing gate and head for Macclesfield Forest.

3 Entering the forest, locate the green information post signposted Langley and continue downhill following signs for Trentabank along a gravel footpath until you reach Trentabank Reservoir car park and Ranger centre in the middle of Macclesfield Forest.

4 From the Ranger centre turn left along the road for 200m, then bear right at a fork. When you reach Ridgegate Reservoir take the new concessionary path along the southern shore (on your left) which leads all the way round to the Leather's Smithy inn at Langley on the far side. Turn left at the inn and go down Clarke Lane, with Bottoms Reservoir on the right.

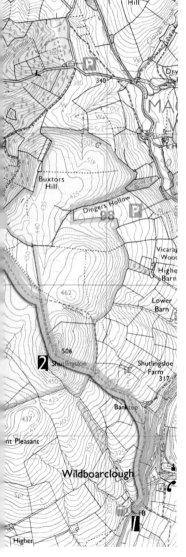

5 Before the end of Bottoms Reservoir branch right at the sign for the Gritstone Trail (indicated by a black bootprint symbol with a letter 'G' on the sole) on to a gravel path which runs parallel to the road. Swing right along the dam wall, over a footbridge and up some steps, emerging at the smaller Teggsnose Reservoir.

Macclesfield Forest

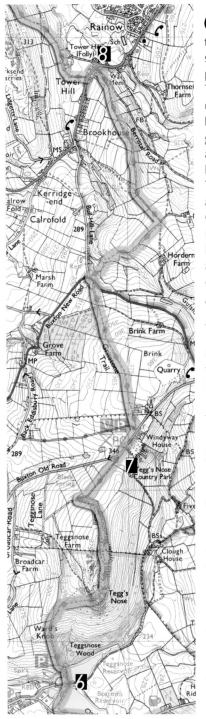

6 Go straight ahead again along the dam wall and at the north west tip of this reservoir, bear left on the steeply stepped Gritstone Trail and past the sign indicating the boundary of Tegg's Nose Country Park. Continue uphill on the main path (ignore paths leading off) until you enter a small flat grassy meadow. Head up slightly right and through a small gate. Turn right here onto a flat gravel track contouring Tegg's Nose among patches of heather, and past some old quarry machinery. Continue through a gate, then bear right at a fork down stone steps with a handrail to a metal gate. Turn right onto a wide track to reach the visitor centre, café and car park.

7 Go out of the visitor centre and turn right along the road, then after 130m go left at the turning and then almost immediately go right into a field, following the Gritstone Trail across hilltop fields. Cross the A537 ('Cat and Fiddle' road) with care, turn left along the pavement and at the T-junction, pick up the Gritstone Trail again and stay on it until you reach the B5470 at Tower Hill Folly in Rainow village.

8 Cross the B5470 and turn left; then after 100m turn right on the Gritstone Trail. Go through a gate downhill, then curve right along a wooded gully. At the end of the wood turn half left, steeply uphill, through meadows and gates until the path levels out on the ridge known as the Saddle of Kerridge. Bear right at a multiple finger post on the Gritstone Trail, all the way along to the small tower known as White Nancy (see next stage for some background to this curiosity).

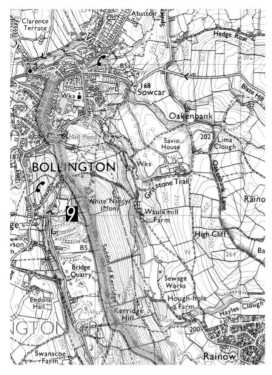

9 Continue beyond White Nancy, steeply downhill on a stone-stepped path. When you reach a crossing track leave the Gritstone Trail and go straight over on the signposted footpath. Go through a kissing gate steeply downhill on a grass field track, through two more metal gates onto a stone-stepped path and through the next field to Bollington, emerging on Lord Street. Turn left, continue for 70m, then turn right into High Street. Head down this to its end, then cross the main road into Pool Bank car park.

View from Tegg's Nose

Take back the tracks

Throughout the Peak District rights of way allow everyone to enjoy the countryside by foot, cycle, horse and motor vehicle, depending on the status of the route. Footpaths are for walkers, bridleways are for walkers, cyclists and horse riders, restricted byways have similar users to bridleways but include horse carriages, and BOATS (Byways Open to All Traffic) and other green lanes of undetermined status are open to everyone, including motorised vehicles.

Friends of the Peak District has always campaigned for a beautiful countryside for everyone to enjoy but until recently had played a supportive, rather than a leading, role in access campaigning. However, in the last 20 years with the easy spread of information through the internet the Peak District's green lanes are being used increasingly by visitors on motor bikes and in 4x4 vehicles from near and far, including from abroad. Such use has escalated to a point where some routes cannot sustain it. Indeed it adds to the enjoyment of these motorised users if such routes are rocky, deeply rutted, muddy and wet and have trees alongside them for winching vehicles out of trouble.

However, these lanes are often part of a network of sensitive medieval routes built for the horse and cart as important trading routes, for example to move salt east from Cheshire to Yorkshire. Good examples of such routes exist throughout the south west Peak and can be found at Hollinsclough and Kerridge (beautifully depicted in Alan Garner's novel 'Thursbitch'), and further north between Bamford and Long Causeway at Hurstclough Lane. These intimate lanes were often cobbled, support a rich diversity of wildlife adjacent to them and offer safe and tranquil routes for local people and visitors to enjoy the countryside. They are also often narrow and steep, with blind bends.

Consequently, motorbike and 4x4

use of them is wholly inappropriate. They damage and destroy the fragile surface and make it impassable for other users. They often veer off-track running over wild flowers and ancient monuments, and rev up to destroy the tranquillity. Some of these users have little consideration for others and intimidate walkers, cyclists and horse riders who may find it impossible to escape the onslaught of a motorbike travelling at 30mph or faster. The noise terrifies children, dogs and horses, and high verges and walls mean there is no refuge for the more vulnerable. Furthermore, repairs are costly and materials such as tarmac planings destroy the 'ancient' feel of a lane. Worse still, it is money down the drain if vehicle users are still allowed to use and re-erode the route.

National park routes incompatible with motorised vehicles

The national park was designated for everyone to enjoy, but whilst we enjoy it we must take care that its special qualities are not harmed and that we do not spoil the enjoyment of others. As the impact of these off-roaders increased, the Friends believes more needs to be done to address the issues and consequently set up the 'Take Back the Tracks' campaign. Traffic regulation orders banning motorised vehicles from these routes substantially reduces the number of off-roaders and allows the police to prosecute those who defy the law. Slowly, we are ensuring that this protection happens. Already vehicles (excluding mobility and farm vehicles) are banned from iconic routes such as Long Causeway, Chapel Gate, the Pennine Bridleway and The Roych. Others will follow and even if we cannot get a national parks-wide ban of such vehicle use, hopefully green lane networks will be so truncated as to be unattractive to off-roaders and can return to their original tranquil character.

Anne Robinson

Upper Goyt Valley

Bollington to Buxton

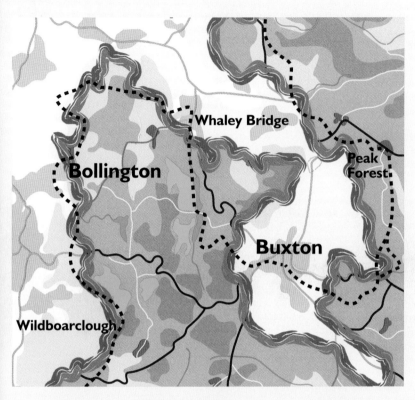

Whaley Bridge

Bollington

Peak Forest

Buxton

Wildboarclough

The last section of the Boundary Walk is as varied as before, beginning in the town of Bollington once famous for cotton spinning and still notable for its mills and chimneys. Although not particularly high, the landscape is rugged and undulating, but then a stretch of canal towpath and the deer park and stately house of Lyme changes the complexion entirely. Whaley Bridge provides a useful final staging post before the Walk swings southwards, reflecting the national park's indented boundary, to trace a route through the Upper Goyt Valley. Past reservoirs and woodland, the Walk makes one last hilltop crossing before a straightforward descent in to Buxton.

Stage 19
Bollington to Whaley Bridge

Start: Bollington (GR SJ 937778)
Finish: Whaley Bridge (GR SK 011814)
OS map: OL 1 Peak District – Dark Peak Area & OL 24 Peak District - White Peak Area
Distance: 9.5 miles/15.3km **Ascent:** 1,363ft/415m

View over Bollington

Paths and terrain: An undulating mix of field paths, hard tracks and lanes, open parkland and even a canal towpath.

What to look out for: At the end of the Saddle of Kerridge, overlooking Bollington, is White Nancy, a Grade II listed bell-shaped monument built in 1817 to commemorate, it is said, the victory at the Battle of Waterloo. On special occasions it has been painted different colours, but is most commonly white. Further on is Lyme Hall, home to the Legh family for 600 years and given to the National Trust in 1946. It featured as Pemberley in the BBC production of 'Pride and Prejudice'.

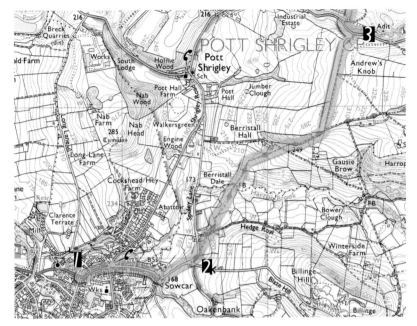

1 Start at Pool Bank car park in Bollington, opposite the Spinners Arms pub. Turn left out of the car park, go uphill and right at the next junction, signposted Rainow, then fork left on Spuley Lane towards Pott Shrigley.

2 Take the footpath on the right through the farm to a track. Turn right on the track uphill, then almost immediately left on the path signposted Gritstone Trail. Pass Berristall Hall and round the foot of the woodland. Go through a gate and straight on with a wall on the left, towards Andrew's Knob.

White Nancy

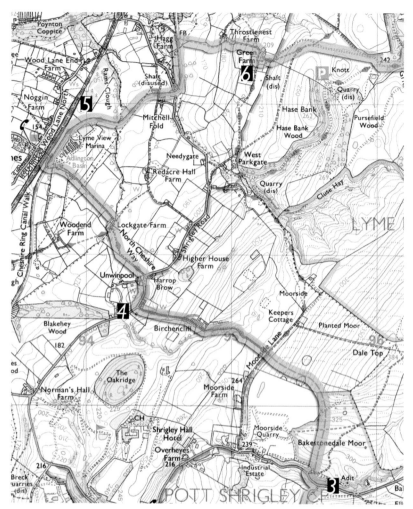

3 Go left on the road then right to the back of the layby, through a gate and up the track. Go through a gate at the top (beyond the interpretation panel about Bollington's industrial heritage of coal mining) and take the path left downhill. Pass the front of a row of houses to the lane ahead.

4 Follow the lane uphill to a footpath on the left, just as the road bends right. After a double stile take the next on the left on to a lane. Continue ahead over the canal bridge where the lane bends right. Take a gated path on your right on to the towpath of the Macclesfield Canal at Lyme View Marina.

5 Walk left along the canal and then cross it at bridge 16, with white ironwork lattice, then walk ahead/right to go through a metal kissing gate. A fenced-in footpath leads uphill to a narrow lane. Turn right into the lane and follow it up until you reach Green Farm on your left.

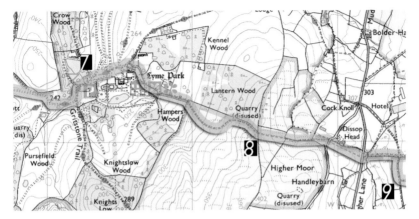

6 Turn sharp left and through a gate alongside the farmyard. At the end of the buildings, turn left and cross the end of the yard for an enclosed path opposite. Cross the ladder stile into the National Trust-owned Lyme Park (and also into the national park). Follow the grass path that leads away diagonally right from the stile all the way down to the main car park.

7 Walk through the car park and up the steps behind the information kiosk. Go past the entrance to the house and follow the bending road past the stable block on the right. Almost immediately go through a gateway (signposted estate vehicles only) to an unsurfaced track. Follow this uphill to cross a large ladder stile and continue uphill on the middle path with a wall and woodland on the left, eventually passing an old quarry on the right.

8 At the top, cross the stone wall stile ahead and downhill over stiles to reach a lane. Cross the stile opposite and on in the same direction over marshy ground. After passing a pond on the left, bear right to reach a stile onto a road. Cross the road through a gate opposite, cross a footbridge and continue uphill to reach a track. Turn right, signposted Kettleshulme.

Bollington to Whaley Bridge

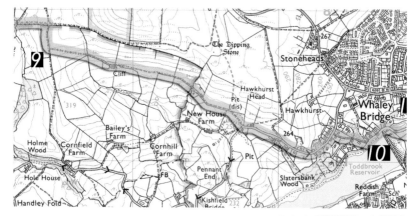

9 Take the footpath on the left (over the stile by side of the gate). Go to the left of the first farm and down to a stream and a gate. Follow the farm track to a tarmac lane and turn left. Go downhill until immediately after Toddbrook bungalow take the walled footpath on the right, down to a road and Toddbrook Reservoir.

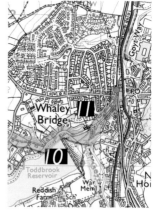

10 Cross the footbridge ahead and turn left on the bridleway. Go up the boat ramp and round the front of the sailing club. Head down through the car park alongside the water gully. Follow the footpath through the park with the stream on your right.

11 At the entrance to the park, turn right on the road and pass under the railway bridge to arrive in the centre of Whaley Bridge.

Lyme House

Stage 20

Whaley Bridge
to Buxton

Start: Whaley Bridge (GR SK 011815)
Finish: Buxton Opera House (GR SK 056734)
OS map: OL 24 Peak District – White Peak Area & OL1 Peak
District – Dark Peak Area
Distance: 9.2 miles/14.8km **Ascent:** 1,216ft/371m

Goyt Valley

Paths and terrain: Very pleasant and straightforward waterside
paths up the Goyt Valley, with one sharp but short climb.
Approaching Buxton, beware golf balls as you cross the golf
course.

What to look out for: Errwood and Fernilee reservoirs were
built by Stockport Corporation Waterworks last century to supply
Greater Manchester's growing population with drinking water,
with farms and houses (including Errwood Hall) demolished to
prevent contamination of the water. Today you can sail on the
water and there are public paths all around. The golf course
you walk across as you enter Buxton was designed by Alister
MacKenzie, who was also responsible for planning the world-
famous Augusta National course in the USA.

1 From Whaley Bridge railway station, take Reservoir Road (signposted Toddbrook Reservoir). Go under the railway bridge and through Whaley Bridge Memorial Park (entrance on the left).

2 Cross the stream over the bridge and take the steep path on the right signposted Reservoir Walk. Go past the BMX park, where the path becomes the Midshires Way. Arrive on a road and follow it through a housing estate. Cross the main road to the footpath ahead and into open fields. Stay on the path (though faint at times), eventually crossing a lane and into woodland.

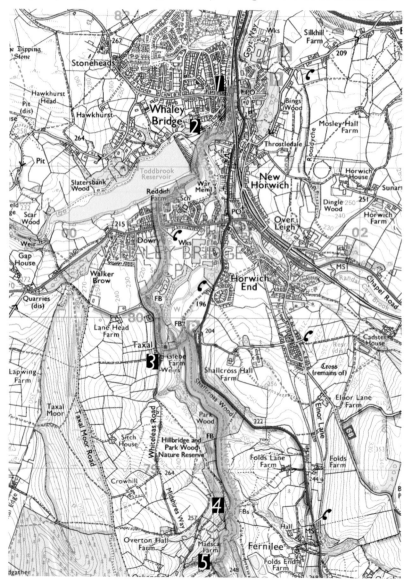

Buxton Pavilion Gardens

3 Emerge on the road at St James Church in Taxal and turn left. Take the first path on left, a restricted byway, between two sections of the graveyard, down to the river. Turn left to cross the bridge then turn right and zigzag left up to a footpath on the right through woods.

4 At a footbridge cross the river and pass the nature reserve entrance, then turn left and cross another footbridge over the river before taking the grassy track uphill, signposted Knipes, until you reach the lane beyond Knipes Farm (Madscar Farm on the OS map).

5 Turn left and follow the lane/track until it crosses a cattle grid. Follow the lane right, with Fernilee Dam on the left. Turn left through a gate into woods, signposted Errwood. Keep left at a fork, then left for the signposted Waterside Walk. Follow the path gently downhill and alongside the reservoir.

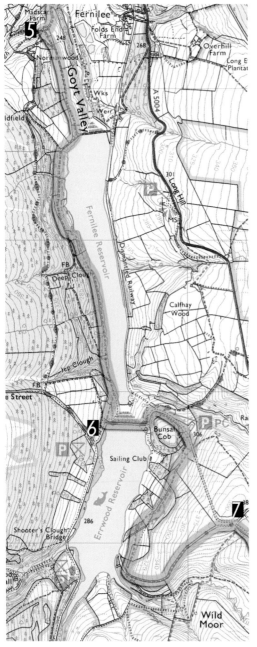

6 At the end ascend right to the road and follow the road over Errwood Dam and on through left and right bends, then uphill to a fingerpost on the right. Turn right and follow the path towards the centre of a belt of trees ahead. Continue through a gate, first with the wall on the left and then across open fields with views over the reservoir to your right. After nearly one kilometer,, by a bench, fork left and go uphill to join the road by a car park and large pond.

7 Turn right and follow the old railway line until you reach the tunnel end. Take the footpath on your left signposted Buxton and Bishop's Lane. Follow this until you approach some trees. Take the left hand fork and descend steps (paid for by HF Holidays Pathways fund) to Bishop's Lane.

8 Turn left on to the lane and head uphill to the front of a row of cottages. Pass to the right of them and through to the woodland at the back. Follow the path down to Watford Farm and go right through a large gate and onto the golf course.

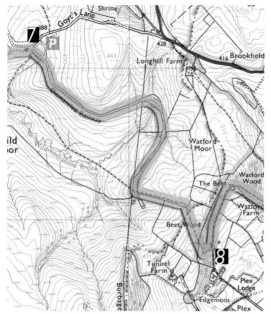

9 Take the wide track (a public footpath) down the middle of the golf course to Watford Road. At the end turn right into Carlisle Road and at the T-junction at the bottom cross St John's Road.

10 Turn left and take the next path on your right into Serpentine Gardens. This then crosses Burlington Road into the Pavilion Gardens. Follow it along to the Opera House then turn right and head uphill to reach the market place.

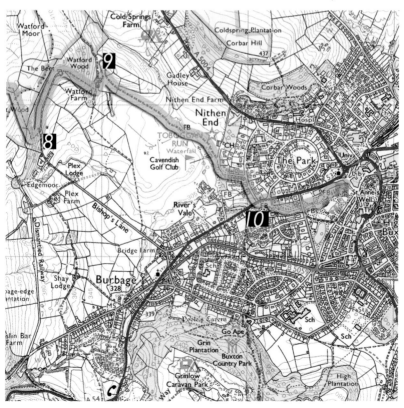

Torrs Hydro, New Mills

The power of water

All landscapes, and especially the Peak District, have been formed and changed by the power of water. The rocks of the Dark and White Peak were laid down in the rivers, deltas and seas of eons past and then carved out by water into the hills and valleys which this Boundary Walk traverses. High rainfall and steep gradients mean the Peak is blessed with a profusion of fast running brooks and rivers. Most in the west of the Peak run all year round, except in times of drought. Peak rivers have been used for mechanical power for 1,000 years – the Domesday Book lists mills at Ashford, Bakewell, Dovedale, Hope, Tissington and Youlgreave in the Derbyshire Peak alone.

Virtually any watercourse would have been used and for myriad purposes: milling corn and other grains, sawing timber, grinding tools and pulverizing minerals, washing cloth and minerals, to name but a few. Even though many of these mill sites are now difficult to find,

they remain a ghostly presence in the landscape through local names such as Waulkmill, near Bollington, to the River Goyt itself, its name coming from a goit (gote or gota in Middle English) meaning a channel of water or stream.

The typical mill comprised an inflow channel ('leat' or 'goit') diverting water from a weir on the stream or river, creating the drop ('head') of water needed to power a wheel. Often, on small streams, the leat would feed a millpond enabling the water to be stored (as potential energy) to allow for a morning's milling or grinding, then stopped up to refill for another period of working the next day. Thus the presence of a millpond can sadly mean a site with low potential for re-development of hydro-electric power in the 21st century.

Water was the main source of rural power from medieval times up to the end of the 19th century. In 1879 the first water turbine that generated electricity was installed at Crag House, in Northumberland. This heralded a switch to electric power that gathered pace in the countryside from the 1920s onwards. In the Peak, a number of mills were converted to turbines, providing either private or local community power. An early pioneer was the electrical engineer and inventor, Sebastian de Ferranti, who converted Baslow Old Mill to provide power for his house, Baslow Hall.

The 20th century also saw the last major water-related change to the Peak's landscapes with the creation of reservoirs on the main south Pennine catchments, including the Goyt. Stockport Corporation bought the Errwood Estate in 1930 and built Fernilee Reservoir in the 1930s and Errwood Reservoir in the 1960s, reducing the power potential of the lower parts of the Goyt for ever. Happily a 150 kilowatt (kW) hydro-electric turbine was installed below Errwood Reservoir in 1989 and downstream, at the confluence with the River Sett in New Mills, the UK's first community hydropower scheme – Torrs Hydro - started generating in 2008.

In recent years, the Friends of the Peak District has been campaigning for the development of appropriately scaled new green energy sources in the national park. The main thrust has been the re-use of old mill infrastructure for micro hydro power. After three years' research, including surveying a dozen mill sites between Bollington and Buxton, the definitive study 'Peak Power' was published in 2010, in collaboration with the Peak District National Park Authority. It concluded that hydro power capacity in the Peak could be at least doubled (up to about 3000 kW). Since then, a small number of mills and other sites have started to produce power again, but much more is still needed.

Andy Tickle

Chatsworth House (South Front)

Peak District Boundary Walk – facilities checklist

Stage	Pub/cafe	Shops	Toilets	Public transport	Accommodation
1 Buxton to Peak Forest	Buxton Peak Forest	Buxton, Blackwell Mill (tuck shop)	Buxton	Buxton (bus, train), Peak Forest (bus)	Buxton, Peak Forest
2 Peak Forest to Hayfield	Peak Forest, Chapel-en-le-Frith (off route), Hayfield	Chapel-en-le-Frith (off route), Hayfield	Chapel-en-le-Frith (off route), Hayfield	Peak Forest (bus), Chapel-en-le-Frith (off route) (bus, train), Hayfield (bus)	Peak Forest, Chapel-en-le-Frith (off route), Hayfield
3 Hayfield to Old Glossop	Hayfield, Birch Vale, Rowarth, Old Glossop	Hayfield, Glossop	Hayfield, Glossop	Hayfield (bus), Glossop (bus, train), Old Glossop (bus)	Hayfield, Rowarth, Old Glossop
4 Old Glossop to Greenfield	Old Glossop, Padfield, Tintwistle, Greenfield	Glossop, Greenfield	Glossop, Dovestone Reservoir	Glossop (bus, train), Old Glossop (bus), Padfield (bus), Hadfield (train), Greenfield (bus, train)	Old Glossop, Padfield
5 Greenfield to Marsden	Greenfield, Pobgreen, Marsden	Greenfield, Marsden	Dovestone Reservoir, Marsden	Greenfield (bus, train), Marsden (bus, train)	Marsden
6 Marsden to Holme	Marsden, Meltham (off route), Holme	Marsden, Meltham (off route), Holme (Fleece Pantry)	Marsden	Marsden (bus, train), Meltham (off route) (bus), Holme (bus)	Marsden, Meltham
7 Holme to Langsett	Holme, Langsett		Langsett	Holme (bus), Dunford Bridge (bus), Hazlehead (bus), Langsett (bus)	Langsett
8 Langsett to Low Bradfield	Langsett, Bolsterstone, High Bradfield, Low Bradfield	Low Bradfield	Langsett	Langsett (bus), Bradfield (bus)	Langsett, Bolsterstone
9 Low Bradfield to Ringinglow	Low Bradfield, Ringinglow	Low Bradfield		Bradfield (bus), Ringinglow (bus)	Ringinglow
10 Ringinglow to Millthorpe	Ringinglow, Millthorpe			Ringinglow (bus), Millthorpe (bus)	Ringinglow

Walk						
11 Millthorpe to Beeley	Millthorpe, Robin Hood, Beeley	Beeley		Millthorpe (bus), Robin Hood (bus), Beeley (bus)	Beeley
12 Beeley to Winster	Beeley, Rowsley, Birchover, Winster	Beeley, Winster		Beeley (bus), Rowsley (bus), Birchover (bus), Winster (bus)	Beeley, Rowsley, Birchover, Winster
13 Winster to Roystone Grange	Winster, Bonsall	Winster, Bonsall		Winster (bus), Bonsall (bus)	Winster, Bonsall
14 Roystone Grange to Thorpe	Parwich, Fenny Bentley, Thorpe	Parwich	Thorpe/Dovedale	Parwich (bus), Fenny Bentley (bus), Thorpe (bus)	Fenny Bentley, Thorpe
15 Thorpe to Waterfall	Thorpe, Ilam Hall, Waterhouses, Waterfall	Waterhouses	Thorpe/Dovedale, Ilam Hall (NT), Waterhouses,	Thorpe (bus), Ilam (bus), Waterhouses (bus)	Thorpe, Ilam YH, Waterhouses
16 Waterfall to Tittesworth Reservoir	Waterfall, Onecote, Upper Hulme, Tittesworth Reservoir Visitor Centre, Meerbrook		Tittesworth Reservoir Visitor Centre	Onecote (bus), Upper Hulme (bus)	Upper Hulme
17 Tittesworth Reservoir to Wildboarclough	Tittesworth Reservoir Visitor Centre, Meerbrook, Wildboarclough		Tittesworth Reservoir Visitor Centre		Wildboarclough
18 Wildboarclough to Bollington	Wildboarclough, Macclesfield Forest/Trentabank, Langley, Tegg's Nose Visitor Centre, Rainow, Bollington	Bollington	Macclesfield Forest/Trentabank, Tegg's Nose Visitor Centre, Bollington	Langley (bus), Tegg's Nose Visitor Centre (bus), Rainow (bus), Bollington (bus)	Wildboarclough, Bollington
19 Bollington to Whaley Bridge	Bollington, Coffee Tavern Shrigley Road, Wood Lanes, Lyme Park, Whaley Bridge	Whaley Bridge	Lyme Park (NT), Whaley Bridge	Bollington (bus), Whaley Bridge (bus, train)	Bollington, Whaley Bridge
20 Whaley Bridge to Buxton	Whaley Bridge, Buxton	Whaley Bridge, Buxton	Whaley Bridge, Buxton	Whaley Bridge (bus, train), Buxton (bus, train)	Whaley Bridge, Buxton

Information correct at time of publication

Last stretch to Buxton at the end of the Peak District Boundary Walk

Photo credits

Thank you to the following who provided photographs for the Boundary Walk book:

Andrew McCloy: pages 4, 26, 28, 38, 40, 51, 65, 94, 97, 102, 114, 121, 129, 131, 133, 136, 142

Bill Bennett: pages 12, 66, 73, 74 80

David Toft: page 17

John Beatty: pages 134, 135

Julie Gough: pages 17, 31, 36, 37, 45, 64, 110, 141

Laurence Hallett: page 139

Paul Maguire: pages 82, 83, 87, 89, 91, 96, 101, 106, 111, 115 124, 128

Phil Sproson: pages 10, 21, 68, 138, 143, 145

Rod Egglestone: page 148

Tim Mackey: Front cover, pages 24, 43, 46, 49, 52, 54, 59, 63, 72, 78, 79x2, 86, 92, 93, 105, 107, 108, 120, 122, 152

FPD/CPRE archives: pages 22, 23

Moors for the Future Partnership: page 50

Chris Sainty: page 51 (bottom)

Villager Jim: Back cover

Acknowledgements

Special thanks to Andrew McCloy (editor) and Tim Mackey (designer) for their commitment to the boundary walk project and particularly for their unstinting hard work on the book. Also particular thanks to Brian Couzins for his amazing support and attention to detail. And to David Gates.

Walk volunteers: Martin Barry, John Bull, Colin Davison, Helen Davison, David Gates, Laurence Hallett, Philip Hetherington, Mary Ann Hooper, David Hurrell, Paul Keetley, Peter Long, Kevin Marsden, Barbara Milton, Gill and Tom North, David Roberts, Ian Salvage, Jill Salvage, David Selkirk, Jody Spilman-Gough, John Temple, Peter Townsend, George Wolfe.

Article writers: John Bull, Paul Keetley, Andrew McCloy, Anne Robinson, John Temple, Andy Tickle, Andrew Wood.

Admin and other volunteers: Lucy Fox, Roderick Lees, Janet Mort, Alison Smith, Sally Taylor, Tina Heathcote, Janet Miller and the Buxton Town Team. And all our members and supporters.

Moors for the Future Partnership: Since 2003, the Moors for the Future Partnership has been working to reverse more than 200 years of damage caused by industrial pollution and wildlife, that left large areas of Peak District and South Pennine uplands bare of vegetation. Works span from Nidderdale to Kinder Scout.

Stamping stations for the official Peak District Boundary Walk passport

www.marstons.co.uk/pubs/finder
www.marstonsinns.co.uk

Pub	Telephone	Accom	Website
Kings Head, **Buxton** SK17 6EJ	01298 27719		kingsheadbuxtonpub.co.uk/
Old Sun, **Buxton** SK17 6HA	01433 51480		
Nineteenth Hole, **Buxton** SK17 7EN	07545 011733		
Fickle Mermaid, **Chapel-en-le-Frith** SK23 0RB	01298 812346		ficklemermaidpub.co.uk
George Hotel, **Hayfield** SK22 2JE	01663 743691	🛏	georgehotelhayfield.co.uk/
Prince of Wales, **Glossop** SK13 8PX	01457 237432		
Swan Inn, **Saddleworth** OL3 5AA	01457 873451		theswandobcross.com/
Kingfisher, **Saddleworth** OL3 7AE	01457 872295		kingfisherpubsaddleworth.co.uk/
Railway, **Marsden** HD7 6DH	01484 841541		
Fleece, **Holme** HD9 2QG	01484 683449	🛏	fleeceinnholme.co.uk/
Robin Hood Inn, **Baslow** DE45 1PQ	01246 583186		robinhoodinnbaslow.co.uk/
Wheatsheaf, **Baslow** DE45 1SR	01246 582240	Marston's	wheatsheafpubbaslow.co.uk
Gate Inn, **Brassington** DE4 4HJ	01629 540448		oldgateinnbrassington.co.uk/
Grouse & Claret, **Rowsley** DE4 2EB	01629 733233	Marston's	grouseclaretpub.co.uk
Bridge, **Ashbourne** DE6 1GF	0133 5418234		thebridgeashbourne.co.uk/
Smiths Tavern, **Ashbourne** DE6 1GH	01335 300809		
Stepping Stones, **Ashbourne** DE6 1AY	01335 300800		steppingstonespub.co.uk
Shady Oak, **Whaley Bridge** SK23 7HD	01663 733658	🛏	
Shepherds Arms, **Whaley Bridge** SK23 7HR	01663 732384		

Passports and completion certificates available at
www.friendsofthepeak.org.uk

Torrs Hydro, New Mills ©Rod Egglestone

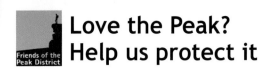

Love the Peak?
Help us protect it

The natural beauty of the Peak District is a source of inspiration, relaxation and recreation for millions of people. The Friends of the Peak District work to protect its beautiful landscape and campaign to support its thriving communities.

Over the years, the Friends' campaigning and influence has shaped the birth of national parks and initiated the creation of green belts nationwide: our predecessors fought against quarries and motorways, racing circuits and sprawling housing; and campaigned for sustainable energy and affordable houses.

Although the unique landscape of the Peak District is now protected by statute it still faces serious threats every day.

Working alongside local communities, we still fight to protect the countryside from urban sprawl, and from damage by illegal off-road vehicles, and we try to persuade developers to improve the environmental impact of their housing schemes and to provide more affordable housing for local residents.

We support wind turbines in some landscapes but campaign against those which would have an unacceptable visual impact on the national park. We also campaign for a living, working countryside which supports sustainable rural economies and remains beautiful forever.

We can't be sure what threats the Peak District will face in the future – unsightly developments, changing economic forces, conflicting demands for land use, a rapidly growing population, new technologies – but we do know that the national park will always need a champion.

As an independent charity, the Friends of the Peak District provide the vigilance and vigorous campaigning needed to ensure that the Peak District's amazing landscapes are safeguarded now and for generations to come.

Over 90 years ago a small and select gathering of like-minded men and women, disturbed by the increasing defacement of the beauty of the Peak District, met to form a society. Gerald and Ethel Haythornthwaite and their friends left us an amazing and lasting legacy. Not only did they provide a blueprint for countryside protection, but also a financial legacy for the Friends to continue their valuable work.

This work is only possible if more people who love the Peak District help us look after it by becoming members.

So if you care about the Peak District, please support the Friends in any way you can. For more information, visit www.friendsofthepeak.org.uk

Solomon's Temple, Buxton ©Phil Sproson

Red grouse ©Rod Egglestone